Mind Control Mastery

BY JEFFREY POWELL

Successful Guide to Human Psychology and Manipulation, Persuasion and Deception!

4th Edition

Table of Contents

Introduction

Are you wondering how you can effectively manipulate, persuade and deceive another person to contribute to your cause, vote for your political candidate, buy your goods or avail of your services? If the answer is yes, this book is definitely for you! The truth is everything that you have right now, and everything that you will ever have, will come from your interactions with other people. Therefore, consciously or unconsciously, you are consistently trying to persuade, manipulate and deceive other people through your words and actions.

I want to thank you and congratulate you for buying this book. "Mind Control Mastery – Successful Guide to Human Psychology and Manipulation, Persuasion and Deception!"

The book contains the most comprehensive techniques of human psychology—manipulation, persuasion and deception—in order to help you in your personal goals. The goal of this book is to provide the reader with techniques, strategies and exercises that they can readily perform. As such, the author of this book has made it possible to create a successful mind-control mastery guide that provides a good working knowledge of the fundamental concepts that is highly practical, instead of being passive and abstract. Moreover, effort has been made to make this reference book as intuitive and easy to learn as possible. This book will be perfect for anyone who wants to improve his or her interactions with another person in a way that will advance his or her goals.

In the first chapter, you will learn the fundamental concepts of human psychology and manipulation, persuasion and deception. In the second chapter, specific tactics for manipulation are outlined. In the third chapter, specific tactics for persuasion are discussed. The specific tactics for deception are outlined as well. You will also learn about the various applications of mind control, particularly in sales and marketing, negotiation and in establishing credibility.

At the end of the day, your skills on manipulation, persuasion and deception will be greatly improved! This will help you get more of what you desire and to do that when you want it and that's a very useful tool for you to have within your life.

Thanks again for buying this book. I hope you enjoy it and gain benefit from it.

Fundamental Thinkers in History of Psychology

Psychology is the study of mental and behavioral processes. Essentially, those who work in the field of psychology try to give meaning to the questions, "What makes you tick?" and "How do you see the world?" These very simple ideas encompass many different and complicated topics, including emotions, thought processes, dreams, memories, perception, personality, illness, and treatment.

While the roots of psychology date back to the philosophers of Ancient Greece, it wasn't until 1879, when German psychologist Wilhelm Wundt created the first laboratory completely devoted to the study of psychology that the field really began to take off. Since then, psychology has expanded exponentially into a truly diverse science, often overlapping with other types of scientific studies such as medicine, genetics, sociology, anthropology, linguistics, biology, and even subjects like sports, history, and love.

Chapter 1: IVAN PAVLOV (1849–1936)

The man who studied man's best friend

Ivan Pavlov was born in Ryazan, Russia, on September 14th, 1849. The son of the village priest, Pavlov originally studied theology until 1870, when he abandoned his religious studies and attended the University of St. Petersburg to study physiology and chemistry.

From 1884 to 1886, Pavlov studied under renowned cardiovascular physiologist Carl Ludwig and gastrointestinal physiologist Rudolf Heidenhain. By 1890, Pavlov had become a skilled surgeon and took an interest in the regulation of blood pressure. Without the use of any anesthesia, Pavlov was able to almost painlessly insert a catheter into a dog's femoral artery and record the impact that emotional and pharmacological stimuli had on blood pressure. However, Pavlov's most influential research with dogs—classical conditioning—was yet to come.

From 1890 to 1924, Ivan Pavlov worked at the Imperial Medical Academy as a professor of physiology. In his first ten years at the academy, he began to turn his attention towards the correlation between salivation and digestion. Through a surgical procedure, Pavlov was able to study the gastrointestinal secretions of an animal during its life span within relatively normal conditions; and he conducted experiments to show the relationship between autonomic functions and the nervous system. This research led to the development of Pavlov's most important concept, the conditioned reflex. By 1930, Pavlov had begun using his research on conditioned reflexes to explain human psychoses.

Though he was praised and supported by the Soviet Union, Pavlov was an outspoken critic of the government's Communist regime and even denounced the government publicly in 1923, following a trip to the United States. When, in 1924, the government expelled the sons of priests at the former Imperial Medical Academy (which was then known as the Military Medical Academy in Leningrad), Pavlov, the son of a priest himself, resigned from his position as professor. Dr. Ivan Pavlov died on February 27th, 1936, in Leningrad.

CLASSICAL CONDITIONING—LEARNING BY ASSOCIATION

Classical conditioning was Ivan Pavlov's most famous and influential work, and it laid much of the groundwork of behavioral psychology. In essence, the idea of classical conditioning is simply learning something by association. Pavlov identified four basic principles:

1. **The Unconditioned Stimulus:** A stimulus is any act, influence, or agent that creates a response. An unconditioned stimulus is when the stimulus automatically triggers some type of response. For example, if pollen makes a person sneeze, then pollen is an unconditioned stimulus.

2. **The Unconditioned Response:** This is a response that is automatically triggered as a result of the unconditioned stimulus. In essence, this is a natural, unconscious reaction to whatever the stimulus might be. For example, if pollen makes a person sneeze, the sneeze is the unconditioned response.

3. **The Conditioned Stimulus:** When a neutral stimulus (a stimulus that is not related to the

response) becomes associated with an unconditioned stimulus, thus triggering conditioned response.

4. **The Conditioned Response:** This is a response that was learned from the once-neutral stimulus.

Confused? Don't be. It's actually very simple! Imagine if you flinched after hearing a loud sound. The sound triggered a natural response, making it an unconditioned stimulus, and the flinching was the unconditioned response because it was something that you did unconsciously as a result of the unconditioned stimulus.

Now, if you repeatedly witnessed a certain movement happen at the same time as, or a little bit before, the loud noise occurred—for example, a person swinging their fist to slam it on a table—you might then begin to associate that movement with the loud sound, flinching whenever you see a fist move in a similar manner, even if there is no sound. The movement of the fist (the conditioned stimulus) became associated with the unconditioned stimulus (the sound), and made you flinch (the conditioned response).

PAVLOV'S DOGS

Dr. Ivan Pavlov was able to establish these ideas by observing the irregular secretions of nonanesthetized dogs. Pavlov initially began studying digestion in dogs by measuring the amount of saliva that the animals had when both edible and nonedible items were introduced.

Eventually, he began to notice that the dogs would begin salivating every time an assistant entered the room. Believing that the animals were responding to the white coats the assistants wore, Pavlov hypothesized that this production of saliva was actually in response to a certain stimulus, and that these dogs were associating the white coats with the presentation of food. Furthermore, Pavlov noted, the production of saliva that occurred when food was presented to the dogs was an unconditioned reflex, while the production of saliva that was a result of the dogs seeing the white coats was a learned, or conditioned, reflex. To dig deeper into his findings, Pavlov set out to create one of the most famous scientific experiments of all time: Pavlov's dogs.

PAVLOV'S DOGS EXPERIMENTAL PROGRESSION

1. The test subjects in this conditioned response experiment are laboratory dogs.
2. First, an unconditioned stimulus must be chosen. In this experiment the unconditioned stimulus is food, which will evoke a natural and automatic response: salivation. For a neutral stimulus, the experiment utilizes the sound of a metronome.
3. Observing the subjects prior to conditioning reveals that saliva is generated when the dogs are exposed to food, and no saliva is generated when the dogs are exposed to the sound of the metronome.
4. To begin the process, the subjects are repeatedly exposed to the neutral stimulus (the sound of the metronome) and are immediately presented with the unconditioned stimulus (food).
5. Over a period of time, the subjects will begin to equate the sound of the metronome to the delivery of food. The longer the experiment progresses, the more deeply ingrained the conditioning will become.
6. After the conditioning phase is completed, the neutral stimulus (the metronome) will cause the subjects to begin salivating in anticipation of food, regardless of whether or not food is presented. Salivation has become a conditioned response.

Even though he is most well known in popular culture for his famous dogs, the importance of Pavlov's research goes far beyond the production of saliva. His revelations on conditioning and learned responses have played a major role in understanding behavioral modification in humans, and in advancing the treatment of such mental health issues as panic disorders, anxiety disorders, and phobias.

Chapter 2: B. F. SKINNER (1904–1990)

It's all about the consequences

Burrhus Frederic Skinner was born on March 20th, 1904, in Susquehanna, Pennsylvania. The son of a lawyer and housewife, Skinner had a warm and stable childhood, and was left with plenty of time for creativity and invention—two traits that would serve him well throughout his career. Having graduated from Hamilton College in 1926, Skinner originally set his sights on becoming a writer. It was while working as a bookstore clerk in New York City that Skinner discovered the works of John B. Watson and Ivan Pavlov, which so fascinated him that he put his plans of becoming a novelist to the side and decided to pursue a career in psychology.

When Skinner was twenty-four years old, he enrolled in the psychology department of Harvard University and began his studies under William Crozier, the chair of the new physiology department. Though not himself a psychologist, Crozier was interested in studying the behavior of animals "as a whole," an approach that was different than the approaches that psychologists and physiologists took at the time. Instead of trying to figure out all of the processes that were occurring inside the animal, Crozier—and subsequently Skinner—was more interested in the animal's overall behavior. Crozier's ideology matched perfectly with the work that Skinner wished to pursue; he was interested in learning how behavior was related to experimental conditions. Skinner's most significant and influential work, the notion of operant conditioning and the invention of the operant conditioning chamber, came out of his days at Harvard. The work Skinner conducted while at Harvard University is still some of the most important research with regards to behaviorism—work which he taught firsthand to generations of students at his alma mater until he passed away at the age of eighty-six, in 1990.

OPERANT CONDITIONING AND THE SKINNER BOX

B. F. Skinner's most important work was the concept of operant conditioning. Essentially, operant conditioning is when someone learns a behavior as the result of the rewards and punishments associated with that behavior. Operant conditioning can be broken down into four types:

1. Positive Reinforcement: This is when a behavior is strengthened and the probability of it recurring increases because a positive condition was the result.
2. Negative Reinforcement: A behavior is strengthened as a result of avoiding or stopping a negative condition.
3. Punishment: This occurs when a behavior is weakened and the probability of the behavior recurring decreases due to a negative condition being the result.
4. Extinction: When a behavior is weakened because the result did not lead to a positive condition or a negative condition.

Positive and negative reinforcement will strengthen a particular behavior, making it more likely to occur, and punishment and extinction will weaken a particular behavior.

To see operant conditioning in action, B. F. Skinner performed a very simple experiment and invented the operant conditioning chamber, which is now often referred to as the Skinner Box.

EXPERIMENT

THE SKINNER BOX AND OPERANT CONDITIONING

1. To conduct the experiment, begin by placing a hungry rat inside of the box. Every time the rat presses a lever inside the box, it will receive a pellet of food. The rat will soon come to learn that by pressing the lever, it will get food (a positive condition), and thus a behavior is strengthened by positive reinforcement.

2. Next, place a rat into the box and then give it a slight electrical shock (a negative condition) to its feet. If the rat presses the lever, the shock will stop. Then send another slight electrical shock to the rat's feet. Once again, when the rat presses the lever, the electrical shock stops. Every time the rat is given an electrical shock, the rat learns that in order to stop it, it must press the lever. This is an example of negative reinforcement, because the rat is learning a behavior in order to stop a negative condition.

3. Place a rat into the box and give it a slight electrical shock (the negative condition) on its feet each time it presses the lever. The behavior of pressing the lever will be weakened because of the negative condition: this is an example of punishment.

4. Now, place the rat into the box and do not give it food or an electrical shock whenever the lever is pressed. The rat will not associate a positive or negative condition to the behavior of pressing the lever, and thus this behavior will be weakened. This is an example of extinction.

THE SKINNER BOX

The Unfortunate Legacy of the Skinner Box

In 1943, Skinner's pregnant wife asked him to build a safer baby crib for their child. Always the inventor, Skinner created a heated crib that was enclosed with a plexiglass window and called it the Baby Tender. Skinner sent an article to *Ladies' Home Journal*, and they printed the story as "Baby in a Box." With the legacy of Skinner's work in operant conditioning, a rumor spread that Skinner had used his experimental operant conditioning chamber on his own daughter and that it eventually drove her crazy to the point of suicide. These rumors, however, were completely false.

SCHEDULES OF REINFORCEMENT

Another important component of operant conditioning is the notion of schedules of reinforcement. How often and when a behavior is reinforced can greatly affect the strength of the behavior and the rate of response. Positive and negative reinforcement can be used, and the goal is always to strengthen behavior and increase the chances of it happening again. Schedules of reinforcement can be broken down into two types:

1. Continuous reinforcement: Every time a behavior occurs, it is reinforced.
2. Partial reinforcement: A behavior is reinforced part of the time.

Interestingly, the response that is the result of partial reinforcement is actually more resistant to extinction because these behaviors are learned over time, and not acquired all at once. Partial reinforcement can be further broken down into four schedules:

1. Fixed-ratio schedules: After a specific number of responses, the response is reinforced. For example, a

rat only gets food pellets after pressing the lever every three times.

2. Variable-ratio schedules: Reinforcement occurs after an unpredictable number of responses. For example, a rat presses the lever several times, but a pellet of food is administered at random and is not based on any sort of fixed schedule.

3. Fixed-interval schedules: A response is rewarded after an allotted period of time. For example, if a rat presses the lever within a time frame of thirty seconds, it will be given one food pellet. It does not matter how many times the rat presses the lever, because only one pellet will be given during that time frame.

4. Variable-interval schedules: Reinforcement occurs after an unpredictable amount of time. For example, the rat may be rewarded a pellet every fifteen seconds, and then every five seconds, and then every forty-five seconds, etc.

Examples of the four different schedules of reinforcement can be found in everyday life. For instance, a fixed-ratio schedule is commonly found in playing videogames (where the player has to collect a certain number of points or coins to obtain a reward); slot machines exhibit a variable-ratio schedule; having a weekly or biweekly paycheck is an example of a fixed-interval schedule; and when one's boss comes into the office to check on an individual's progress at random times, it is an example of a variable-interval schedule. When learning a behavior that is new, a fixed-ratio schedule is always best, while a variable-interval schedule is extremely resistant to extinction.

Though behaviorism lost its popularity over time, there is no denying the impact of B. F. Skinner. His operant techniques remain vital to mental health professionals in helping treat clients, and his ideas of reinforcement and punishment are still used in teaching and dog training.

Chapter 3: SIGMUND FREUD (1856–1939)

The creator of psychoanalysis

Sigmund Freud was born on May 6th, 1856, in Freiberg, Moravia, now the Czech Republic. Freud's mother was his father's second wife, and she was twenty years younger than his father. Freud had two older half-brothers that were around twenty years older than he was; also, he was the first of seven children from his mother. At the age of four, Freud moved from Moravia to Vienna, Austria, where he would spend the majority of his life, despite having claimed to dislike the city.

Freud did well in school, and because he was Jewish—though he later came to identify as an atheist—he attended medical school at the University of Vienna in 1873 (medicine and law were the only viable options available to Jewish men at that time in Vienna). Though Freud wished to pursue neuropsychological research, research positions were extremely hard to come by. As a result, Freud moved into private practice with a focus in neurology.

While training, Freud befriended a physician and psychologist by the name of Josef Breuer. This relationship would prove to be incredibly important to the development of Freud's work once Breuer began treating hysteria patients by using hypnosis and encouraging them to talk about their past. The process of hypnosis, which Breuer's patient Anna O. referred to as "the talking cure," allowed patients to discuss memories that they could not recall during a conscious state; and as a result, the symptoms of their hysteria would be relieved. Freud co-authored *Studies in Hysteria* with Breuer, and then traveled to Paris to learn more about hypnosis under the renowned French neurologist Jean-Martin Charcot.

In 1886, Freud returned to Vienna and began a private practice. Originally, Freud used hypnosis on his neurosis and hysteria patients, but he soon realized that he could get more out of patients by having them sit in a relaxed position (like on a couch) and by encouraging them to say whatever was on their mind (known as free association). By doing so, Freud believed he would be able to analyze what was said and determine what traumatic event in the past was responsible for the patient's current suffering.

Freud's most famous works came in quick succession—in the span of five years, he released three books that would impact psychology for decades to come: 1900's *The Interpretation of Dreams*, in which he introduced the world to the idea of the unconscious mind; 1901's *The Psychopathology of Everyday Life*, where he theorized that slips of the tongue—later known as Freudian slips—were actually meaningful comments revealed by the "dynamic unconscious"; and 1905's *Three Essays on the Theory of Sexuality*, where among other things, he spoke of the now-famous Oedipus complex.

A leading scientific mind of his day, Freud found himself gaining unwanted attention when, in 1933, the Nazi regime came to power in Germany and began burning his works. In 1938, the Nazis seized Austria and Freud had his passport confiscated. It was only due to his international fame and the influence of foreigners that Freud was allowed to move to England, where he remained until his death in 1939.

STAGES OF PSYCHOSEXUAL DEVELOPMENT

Freud's theory of psychosexual development is one of the most well-known and controversial theories in psychology. Freud believed that personality was, for the most part, established by the time a person was six years old and that when a predetermined sequence of stages was successfully completed, it would result in a healthy personality, while failure to do so would lead to an unhealthy personality.

Freud believed that the stages in the sequence were based on erogenous zones (sensitive parts of the body that arouse sexual pleasure, desire, and stimulation) and that failure to complete a stage would make a child fixated on that erogenous zone. This would lead the person to over- or underindulge once he or she was an adult.

Oral Stage (birth–eighteen months)

In this stage, a child focuses on oral pleasures like sucking because they create a sense of comfort and trust. If there is too little or too much gratification in this stage, the child will develop an oral personality or oral fixation and become preoccupied with oral behaviors. According to Freud, people with this type of personality are more likely to bite their nails, smoke, drink, or overeat, and will be gullible, depend on other people, and will always be followers.

Anal Stage (eighteen months–three years)

During this stage, a child's main focus turns towards bladder and bowel control, and a child gains pleasure from controlling these activities. Freud believed that success was achieved in this stage as a result of parents using praise and rewards while toilet training, leaving their child feeling capable and productive—such behavior would lead to the child having a competent, creative personality later on in life. If parents were too lenient to the child during toilet training, he believed, it could lead to an anal-expulsive personality and the child would be destructive, messy, and wasteful. If the parents took an approach that was too strict, or forced toilet training too soon, this could lead to an anal-retentive personality, and the child would develop an obsession with perfection, cleanliness, and control.

Phallic Stage (three–six years)

At this stage, Freud believed the pleasure zones turn towards the genitals, giving rise to one of his most famous ideas, that of the Oedipus complex. Freud believed that, at this stage, a boy unconsciously develops a sexual desire for his mother, sees his father as competition for her affection, and wishes to replace his father. Additionally, the boy will develop castration anxiety as he begins to view his father as someone who is trying to punish him for his Oedipal feelings. Rather than fight with the father, however, the boy will identify with him in an effort to vicariously posses the mother. Fixation at this stage, Freud believed, could lead to sexual deviance and being confused about or having a weak sexual identity.

In 1913, Carl Jung coined the term the "Electra complex," which describes a similar relationship that young girls experience with their fathers. Freud disagreed with this concept, however, believing that girls were actually experiencing penis envy (where resentment and discontent exist because the girls wish that they, themselves, had a penis).

Latency Stage (six years–puberty)

At this stage, sexual urges are suppressed and the sexual energy of the child is directed towards other exchanges like social interactions and intellectual activities. It is during this stage that children play mostly with children of the same sex, and there is no psychosexual development or fixation that occurs.

Genital Stage (puberty–adulthood)

The last stage in Freud's model involves the reawakening of sexual urges and a sexual interest in the opposite sex. If all of the previous stages were completed successfully, the person will be caring and well-balanced, and pleasure will be focused on the genitals. If there is fixation at this stage, the individual may have sexual perversions.

Of course, Freud's theory does have its critics. Freud focused almost exclusively on the development of the male. His research was not based on the behavior of children, but rather on what he was told by his adult patients. Because of the long delay between the hypothetical childhood "cause" and the eventual adulthood "effect" in his theories, it is incredibly difficult to measure or test whether Freud's ideas of psychosexual development are accurate.

STRUCTURAL MODELS OF PERSONALITY

In addition to his conceptions of psychosexual development, Freud believed that there were numerous other driving forces at play that were important to understanding the development of a person's personality. His structural model of personality attempts to describe how the mind works by making distinctions between three parts of personality and the human mind: the id, the ego, and the superego.

Id

Every person is born with an id—the id is responsible for getting the newborn child's basic needs met. Freud claimed that the id is based on something known as a "pleasure principle," which essentially means the id wants whatever feels good at that precise moment and disregards any ramifications. There is no consideration for how the rest of the situation might play out, or for any other people involved. For example, when a baby is hurt, wants something to eat, needs to be changed, or simply wants the attention of others, the id drives the baby to cry until its needs are met.

Ego

The next aspect of the personality—the ego—begins developing naturally over the first three years as a result of the child interacting with the world around him. Because of this, Freud claimed that the ego is based on something he referred to as a "reality principle." The ego comes to realize that there are other people around that also have desires and needs, and that impulsive, selfish behavior can actually lead to harm. The ego has to consider the reality of any particular circumstance while also meeting the needs of the id. For example, when a child thinks twice about doing something inappropriate because he understands the negative outcome that will occur, this is the ego asserting itself.

Superego

The superego develops when a child is five years old and is nearing the end of the phallic stage. This is the part of our personality that is made up of morals and ideals that have been acquired and placed on us by society and our parents. Many people also find the superego to be equivalent to the conscience, since both terms have come to refer to the part of our personality that judges what is right from what is wrong.

Freud believed that, in a truly healthy person, the ego would be stronger than the id and superego so that it could consider the reality of the situation, while both meeting the needs of the id and making sure the superego was not disturbed. In the case of the superego being strongest, a person will be guided by very strict morals, and if the id is strongest, a person will seek pleasure over morality and could end up causing great harm (rape, for example, is when one chooses pleasure-seeking over morality, and is a sign of a strong id).

FREUD'S CONCEPTION OF THE HUMAN PSYCHE

Freud believed that our feelings, beliefs, impulses, and underlying emotions were buried in our unconscious, and therefore not available to the waking mind. However, Freud also believed that there were levels of consciousness beyond just conscious or unconscious. To better understand Freud's theory, imagine an iceberg.

The water surrounding the iceberg is known as the "nonconscious." This is everything that has not become part of our conscious. These are things we have not experienced and are not aware of, and therefore, they do not become part of or shape our personalities in any way.

The tip of the iceberg, our conscious, is only a very small portion of our personality, and since it's the only part of ourselves that we're familiar with, we actually know very little of what makes up our personality. The conscious contains thoughts, perceptions, and everyday cognition.

Directly below the conscious, at the base of the iceberg, is the preconscious or subconscious. If prompted, the preconscious mind can be accessed, but it is not actively part of our conscious and requires a little digging. Things such as childhood memories, our old telephone number, the name of a friend we had when we were younger, and any other deeply stored memories are found in this area. It is in the preconscious mind that the superego can be found.

Since we are only aware of the tip of the iceberg at any given time, the unconscious is incredibly large and consists of those buried, inaccessible layers of our personality. It is here that we find things like fears, immoral urges, shameful experiences, selfish needs, irrational wishes, and unacceptable sexual desires. This is also where the id can be found. The ego is not fixed to one particular part of the iceberg and can be found in the conscious, preconscious, and unconscious.

THE ICEBERG METAPHOR

There is no denying just how influential Sigmund Freud was to the fields of psychology and psychiatry. His ideas completely changed the way people viewed personality, sexuality, memory, and therapy, and he is perhaps the most well-known psychologist in the popular vernacular a century after he first arrived as a notable scholar of the mind.

Chapter 4: ANNA FREUD (1895–1982)

Think about the kids

Anna Freud was born on December 3rd, 1895, in Vienna, Austria, and was the youngest of Sigmund Freud's six children. Though she felt distant with her siblings and mother, Anna was very close with her father. While she did attend a private school, she claimed to have learned very little in class and that much of her education came from being around her father's friends and associates.

Following high school, Freud began translating her father's work into German and working as an elementary school teacher, where she began to take an interest in child therapy. In 1918, Anna contracted tuberculosis and had to leave her teaching position. During this trying time, she began giving her father accounts of her dreams. As he began to analyze her, Anna quickly cemented her interest in her father's profession and decided to pursue psychoanalysis on her own. Although Anna Freud believed in many of the basic ideas that her father did, she was less interested in the structure of the subconscious and more interested in the ego and the dynamics, or motivations, of one's psyche. This interest led to the publication of her groundbreaking book, *The Ego and Mechanisms of Defense*, in 1936.

Anna Freud is perhaps best known for creating the field of child psychoanalysis, which provided great insight into child psychology; she is also recognized for developing different methods to treat children. In 1923, without ever earning a college degree, Freud began her own children's psychoanalytic practice in Vienna and was named as the chair of the Vienna Psycho-Analytic Society.

In 1938, Anna Freud and her family fled the country and moved to England as a result of the Nazi invasion. In 1941, she founded an institution in London with Dorothy Burlingham and Helen Ross called the Hampstead War Nursery, which served as a foster home and psychoanalytic program for homeless children. Her work with the nursery led to three books: *Young Children in Wartime* in 1942, and both *Infants without Families* and *War and Children* in 1943. In 1945, the nursery closed down and Anna Freud created and served as director of the Hampstead Child Therapy Course and Clinic, a role she maintained until her death. By the time she passed away in 1982, Anna had left a lasting and deep legacy on the field that was possibly only overshadowed by the monumental impact of her father and a handful of other psychologists.

DEFENSE MECHANISMS

To understand Anna Freud's contributions to the notion of defense mechanisms, we must first take a look at the work of her father. Sigmund Freud described certain defense mechanisms the ego uses when dealing with conflicts with the id and superego. He claimed that a reduction of tension is a major drive for most people, and that this tension was largely caused by anxiety. Furthermore, he broke anxiety up into three types:

Reality anxiety:
the fear of real-world events occurring. For example, a person is afraid of being bitten by a dog because they are near a ferocious dog. The easiest way to reduce the tension of reality anxiety is to remove oneself from the situation.

Neurotic anxiety:
the unconscious fear that we will be overpowered by and lose control of the urges of the id, and that this will lead to punishment.

Moral anxiety:
the fear of our moral principles and values being violated, resulting in feelings of shame or guilt. This type of anxiety comes from the superego.

When anxiety occurs, Sigmund Freud claimed that defense mechanisms are used to cope with the anxiety and shield the ego from reality, the id, and the superego. He said that oftentimes these mechanisms unconsciously distort reality and can be overused by a person to avoid a problem. It can therefore be beneficial to understand and uncover these defense mechanisms so that a person may manage their anxiety in a healthier way.

But where does Anna Freud come into play? Most notably, she is responsible for identifying the specific defense mechanisms that the ego uses to reduce tension. They are:

Denial:
Refusing to admit or recognize that something is occurring or has occurred

Displacement:
Taking one's feelings and frustrations out on something or someone else that is less threatening

Intellectualization:
Thinking about something from a cold and objective perspective so that you can avoid focusing on the stressful and emotional part of the situation

Projection:
Taking your own uncomfortable feelings and attaching them to someone else so it seems as though that person is feeling that way in place of you

Rationalization:
While avoiding the actual reason for a feeling or behavior, a person will create credible, but false, justifications

Reaction Formation:
Behaving in the opposite way to hide one's true feelings

Regression: reverting back to childlike behavior. Anna Freud claimed that a person would act out certain behaviors based on the stage of psychosexual development that they were fixated on. For example, a person stuck in the oral stage might begin to eat or smoke excessively, or become more verbally aggressive

Repression:
Moving thoughts that make us uncomfortable into our subconscious

Sublimation: converting unacceptable behaviors into a more acceptable form. For example, a person with rage takes up boxing as a way to vent. Sublimation, Freud believed, was a sign of maturity

CHILD PSYCHOANALYSIS

To create a successful therapy for children, Anna Freud originally planned on using her father's work as a guide, so that she could make a timeline and map out a normal rate of growth and development for children. That way, if certain developments, such as hygiene, for example, had been missing or lagging, a therapist could pinpoint the cause to a specific trauma and could then use therapy to address it.

However, Anna quickly came to realize that there were major differences between children and the adult patients her father had seen, and her techniques had to continually change. Whereas Sigmund Freud's patients were self-reliant adults, Anna Freud dealt with children, for whom a major part of their lives involved the presence of their parents. Freud saw the importance of the parents early on; still, a major aspect of child therapy includes parents taking on an active role in the therapy process. For example, parents are generally informed of exactly what goes on during therapy so that they are able to apply the techniques from therapy in everyday life.

Anna Freud also saw the usefulness that child's play could have in therapy. Children could use playing as a means to adapt their reality or confront their problems, and could speak freely during therapy. While play may help a therapist identify a child's trauma and treat it, it doesn't reveal much from the unconscious mind because unlike adults, children have not learned to cover up and repress events and emotions. When a child says something, they mean it!

While she may have begun her career under her father's shadow, Anna Freud proved that she too was an incredibly valuable asset to the world of psychology. Her contributions to her father's work on defense mechanisms and, most importantly, the creation of child psychoanalysis remain extremely important and influential, and a great deal of what we understand about child psychology comes from her work.

Chapter 5: LAWRENCE KOHLBERG(1927–1987)

Moral dilemma

Lawrence Kohlberg was born to a wealthy family in Bronxville, New York, on October 25th, 1927. When World War II came around, Kohlberg enlisted as a sailor with the merchant marines—a decision that would prove to have a major impact on him, and subsequently on the field of psychology.

As a sailor, Kohlberg worked on a freighter and helped smuggle Jewish refugees through a British blockade located in Palestine. This would be the first time Kohlberg took an interest in moral reasoning; and, later on in life, he would return to what is now Israel to study more about the moral reasoning of children growing up in kibbutzes (agricultural communities in Israel based on collectivist principles). When he returned from the war, he attended the University of Chicago and studied psychology. Kohlberg scored so highly on his admissions tests that he did not have to take many of the required courses, and he earned his bachelor's degree in psychology in one year. He then earned his PhD in 1958. By 1967, Kohlberg was a professor of education and social psychology at Harvard University, and became widely known and respected with the creation of his theory of the "stages of moral development."

In 1971, Kohlberg was working in Belize when he contracted a parasitic infection. As a result of the disease, Kohlberg spent the next sixteen years of his life battling depression and constant, debilitating pain. On January 19th, 1987, Kohlberg requested a day of leave from the hospital where he was undergoing treatment. After leaving the hospital,

Kohlberg drowned himself in Boston Harbor. He was fifty-nine years old.

STAGES OF MORAL DEVELOPMENT

Kohlberg's theory on the stages of moral development was a modification of the work performed by Jean Piaget, the Swiss psychologist. While Piaget described moral development as a two-stage process, Kohlberg identified six stages within three levels. Kohlberg proposed that moral development was a process that continued throughout a person's lifespan. In order to isolate and describe these stages, Kohlberg presented a series of difficult moral dilemmas to groups of young children of different ages. He then interviewed them to find out the reasoning behind each of their decisions, and to see how moral reasoning changed as children grew older.

The Heinz Dilemma

In the Heinz Dilemma, Kohlberg told children a story about a woman in Europe who is near death because she has a special type of cancer. The doctors believe there is one drug that might save her: a form of radium recently discovered by the druggist of that same town. Though it is expensive to make the drug, the druggist is charging ten times what it costs to make. He paid $200 and is charging $2,000 for a small dose. Heinz, the sick woman's husband, tries to borrow money from everyone that he knows but only manages to get $1,000—half of what the druggist is charging. Heinz tells the druggist of his dying wife and asks him if he is willing to sell it at a cheaper price or allow Heinz to pay him back later, but the druggist refuses, saying he discovered the drug and will make money from it. Heinz, desperate, breaks into the druggist's store to steal the drug for his wife. Kohlberg then poses the question, "Should the husband have done that?"

The answers to the dilemmas were not as important to Kohlberg as the reasoning behind the decisions. Based on his research, the children's responses were classified into three levels and six stages.

Level 1: Preconventional Morality

Stage 1: Obedience and Punishment

In this stage, children view rules as absolutes. Obeying the rules means avoiding punishment. This stage of moral development is particularly common in younger children, though adults can express this reasoning as well.

Stage 2: Individualism and Exchange

In this stage, children begin to take individual points of view into consideration and judge actions based on how the needs of the individual are served. In the case of the Heinz dilemma, children argued that the choice that best served Heinz's needs was the best course of action.

Level 2: Conventional Morality

Stage 3: Interpersonal Relationships

In this stage, children focus on living up to expectations set by society or the people close to them. In other words, it is important to be good and nice. For this reason, this is also known as the "good boy–good girl" orientation.

Stage 4: Maintaining Social Order

At this stage, society as a whole is taken into consideration. This means there is a focus on following the rules to maintain law and order—even in extreme situations—respecting authority, and fulfilling a duty that one has agreed to do.

Level 3: Post conventional Morality

Stage 5: Social Contract and Individual Rights
In this stage, it becomes understood that people have different beliefs, opinions, and values, and that in order to maintain society, rules of the law should be based on standards that are agreed upon.

Stage 6: Universal Principles
The final stage is based on following internal principles of justice and ethics, even if this means going against what the rules and laws state.

It is important to note that Kohlberg believed that it was only possible to pass through these stages in this order and that not every person achieved all of these stages.

CRITICISMS TO THE STAGES OF MORAL DEVELOPMENT

While extremely important and influential, Kohlberg's model has faced criticism. It has been argued that Kohlberg's work reflected a bias towards males (he claimed most men to be at a stage 4 and most women to be at a stage 3), that there is a notable difference between what a person says they ought to do and what they actually end up doing, and that Kohlberg focused solely on justice but did not take into consideration things like compassion and caring. The way Kohlberg performed his experiment has even been brought into question, due to the fact that he interviewed different children of different ages instead of interviewing the same children over a longer period of time. Regardless, Kohlberg's work in morality remains incredibly influential, and the ideas he set forth are commonly applied to the field of education and are used to understand the behavior of children.

Chapter 6: STANLEY MILGRAM (1933–1984)

A truly shocking psychologist

Stanley Milgram was born on August 13th, 1933, to a Jewish family in New York City. His father was a Hungarian baker and his Romanian mother took over the bakery following his death in 1953. Milgram had always excelled academically and, while attending James Monroe High School, he became active in the school theatre productions. This theatrical experience would prove influential to Milgram, who utilized his background later on in life when creating the realistic experiments he is now most famous for.

In 1953, after graduating from Queens College, New York, with a bachelor's degree in political science, Milgram applied to Harvard University to earn his PhD in social psychology. Though he was initially rejected for having no academic background in psychology, Milgram was finally accepted to Harvard in 1954 and earned his PhD in social psychology in 1960.

In his professional career, Milgram had a strong focus on social issues. From 1959 to 1960, Milgram studied under psychologist Solomon Asch, who was famous for his disturbing experiments on social conformity. In 1961, Milgram would begin his famous obedience study, which remains one of the most infamous and influential psychological experiments ever performed.

In the fall of 1960, Milgram worked as an assistant professor at Yale, and from 1963 to 1966, he was an assistant professor in Harvard's Department of Social Relations. In 1967, Milgram became a lecturer at Harvard; however he was denied tenure, which was likely the result of his controversial Milgram Experiment. That same year, he became a tenured professor at the City University of New York Graduate Center. On December 20th, 1984, Stanley Milgram suffered from a heart attack and died in New York City. He was fifty-one years old.

MILGRAM'S OBEDIENCE STUDY

Stanley Milgram is perhaps most well-known for his famous, yet extremely controversial, experiment on obedience. Milgram was fascinated by the effect that authority had on obedience, and believed that people would nearly always obey orders out of a desire to seem cooperative or out of fear, even if this meant going against their better judgment or desires.

Fitting Milgram's Experiment in History

Milgram began his obedience experiment in 1961. Shortly before, the world had been captivated by the trial of Nazi war criminal Adolf Eichmann, who, among other things, was charged with ordering the deaths of millions of Jews. Eichmann's defense in the case was that he was just following instructions.

Milgram conducted the experiment at Yale University, where he recruited forty men through newspaper ads. The participants were informed (falsely) that the study they were joining was focused on memory and learning. They were told that one person would take on the role of teacher and the other would take on the role of student, and that these roles would be chosen randomly. Each participant drew a supposedly random slip of paper. In reality, however, all of the papers said "teacher" on them. The only "students" were actor accomplices of Milgram's. Thus, all of the unknowing participants were intentionally given the role of the teacher, while believing it to be a random assignment.

EXPERIMENT

MILGRAM'S EXPERIMENT

A VISUALIZATION OF MILGRAM'S EXPERIMENT

1. Each participant "teacher" is paired with one of the accomplice "students." The teacher watches as the student is strapped to a chair and has electrodes attached to him by laboratory assistants.
2. Following this, the teacher is then brought into a separate room, where he can still communicate with the student, but they cannot see each other. The teacher is placed in front of a "shock generator" that starts at 30 volts and increases—in increments of 15 volts—all the way to 450 volts. The switches are labeled "Moderate," which is 75–120 volts; "Strong," which is 135–180 volts; "Danger: Severe Shock," which is 375–420 volts; and the two highest levels are labeled "XXX." The "shock generator" does not produce actual shocks, but rather makes a noise when switches are pressed.
3. The teacher is told that he will teach word pairs to the student and that if the student makes a mistake, the teacher will punish the student by administering a shock. For every mistake made, the teacher must administer a shock 15 volts higher than the last. To show that the experiment is real, the teacher is given a 15 volt shock. This is the only real shock administered in the entire test.
4. The word pairings begin, and the student will eventually begin to make planned errors. At each error,

the teacher increases the voltage of the shock that he gives to the student. When the fake shocks reach 75 volts, the "student" will grunt. At 120 volts, the student will complain that the shocks are painful. At 150 volts, the student will scream that he wants to be released. The student will then plead more and more as the shocks are "administered" and complain that he suffers from a heart condition.

5. If at any time the teacher questions the process, the experimenter will tell him things like "please continue," "it is absolutely essential that you continue," "the experiment requires that you continue," or "you have no other choice, you must go on."
6. At 300 volts, the student pounds on the walls and exclaims that he can't stand the pain. At 330 volts, the student remains quiet. The experimenter informs the teacher that a lack of response is a wrong answer, and that he has to shock the student.
7. The experiment ends when the highest level on the shock generator is reached.

MILGRAM'S FINDINGS

Milgram asked a group of Yale students to predict how many people they thought would administer the maximum shock level, and they estimated three out of 100 people would do it. Surprisingly, Milgram found that 65 percent of the participants in his study administered shock levels of 450 volts! While people did show signs of internal struggle through groaning, nervous laughter, and trembling, most of them obeyed the experimenter's request to continue with the experiment. When interviewed after the experiment, Milgram asked the participants to rate how painful they believed the shocks actually were, and "extremely painful" was the typical answer. Milgram even found that the participants—in an effort to justify their behavior—devalued the student during the experiment, saying the student was so dumb that he actually deserved the shock. Milgram was able to successfully show that under certain circumstances, everyday people who are considered "normal" have the capability to cause intense pain and suffering. Milgram was able to explain such high levels of obedience in the following ways:

- Compliance was increased because of the physical presence of an authority figure (the experimenter)
- Many participants believed the experiment was safe because it was sponsored by Yale
- The selection process of who would be teacher and who would be student seemed random
- It was assumed that the experimenter was a competent expert
- The participants were told the shocks were painful but not dangerous

Chapter 7: Analyzing Different Personality

Did you know the structure of a man's body can tell you more about what he thinks and does than the average mother knows about her own child? While it may sound strange, there is a lot that can be learned from reading people.

Once you learn these techniques, you will never look at anyone quite the same! This principle is based on the idea that every single thought you think has some kind of muscular contraction to go along with it.

What this tells us is our physiology and our psychology is interwoven. The next time you get angry try looking in the mirror to see how your anger affects your facial expressions.

These tendencies and preferences are thought to be inborn and with us from childhood to death. What this means is there is a lot to be learned from studying people and their facial expressions and body movements.

Each of these unique types is a result of the development of the five biological systems in human beings:

- Nutritive
- Circulatory
- Muscular
- Bony
- Nervous

These five types are known as the:

1. The Alimentive Type or the Enjoyer.
2. The Thoracic Type or the Thriller.
3. The Muscular Type or the Worker.
4. The Osseous Type or the Stayer.
5. The Cerebral Type or the Thinker.

Many people are actually a combination of different parts of these types, but you will notice that people tend to be lean more to one particular type over another.

Reading other people by analyzing their unique type, can be a lot of fun. The rules put in place are accurate and based on scientific data, and they work, all the time, under any and all conditions.

The Alimentive Type or the Enjoyer.

This personality type is known for their physical rotundity. They may appear round or circular and have small hands and feet. They may display round fingers and round feet, and have a round waist. They may find it difficult to move with ease they are susceptible to the cold weather.

This type lives to eat and loves being flirtatious and they are usually very popular socially. This type also loves comfort and enjoying life.

The Ailmentive or the Enjoyer is born for business. They can probably sell almost anything, because of the fact that they like the comforts money brings them, so they may tend to attract fields that are high paying.

The Thoracic Type or the Thriller.

This type is known for their red face and high chest. They may also have a long waist. This face may be kite-shaped or wide through the cheekbones, tapering up the sides of the forehead. This type of person is nimble and quick, often walking with a spring in their step. Anyone who is prone to fidgeting may also fall in this category.

This type may be a born entertainer or a lover of the stage and they are known for being clever, dazzling and magnetic.

The Muscular Type or the Worker.

The worker tends to be very muscular and solid. His body shape may be based on the square. He could be short and stocky or just very muscular and he might have longer than normal arms.

This person may appear to have a square head or a thick neck and they might even have a square jaw or square shaped fingers. This type of person is known for their ability to work with their hands.

The Osseous Type or the Stayer.

This type may have a bony appearance or a raw-boned appearance. They may also appear rugged and powerful because of their large joints and angular hands.

This type may also appear oblong in nature with knotty fingers and hands. The Osseous or the Stayer enjoys working on their own without the supervision of other people. The best word to describe this type of person is independent. If left alone, they make excellent employees.

The Cerebral Type or the Thinker.

This type is known for their large head on a small body. They are more prone to mental pursuits than physical and they may even forget to eat. Their face may also be triangular in nature with the widest part of their head closer to the top. Their fingers are smooth and their hands are delicate.

The Cerebral or the Thinkers are born writers and they love working with ideas. Since they are prone to daydreaming, they may be impractical and get lost in thought. This type enjoys meditating, dreaming, visualizing, planning, and anything that involves their wonderful brain.

The Thinker may get involved in writing, library work, education or teaching.

Chapter 8: Kinesics and the Types of Gestures

Kinesics

Stemming from the root word kinesis, meaning movement, Kinesics is the study of actions, particularly those of the face, the hands, the arms, and the body. It is concerned with understanding a person's nonverbal speech through his posture, gestures, facial expressions, and the movement of his head.

Types of Gestures

Adaptors

Have you ever seen a recording of yourself and noticed performing body movements that you weren't aware of doing? These subconscious behaviors are called adaptors. Often, they are the products of anxiety or an overall sense that you are in an unfamiliar environment or situation. These movements may be directed toward oneself, towards others, or towards objects in the surroundings. An example of an adaptor directed towards oneself is when a person fidgets with his fingers or plays with his hair. Unconsciously touching something in your pocket while you are speaking is an example of an adaptor directed towards an object. Try observing people as they wait in a queue and you might see some of them performing subconscious actions like shaking their legs or checking their phones or picking invisible lint from their clothes. This is a person's way of utilizing their excess energy. By understanding adaptors, you will be able to understand a person's internal state.

Emblems

If you've ever seen a hitchhiker, you'll notice that they don't need to say anything to indicate that they need a ride. In fact, the raised thumb says it all. Likewise, in some cultures, a person need not say anything except to raise his middle finger in order to insult someone. These particular hand gestures are called emblems. They refer to movements that have a generally agreed-on implication. Though not a part of an official sign system, most people of a particular culture are able to catch their meaning. Emblems may be used to display emphatic bonds between members of a certain group. In a way, this type of gesture has been invented by people to create some common ground.

Illustrators

These types of gestures are utilized by the speaker to aid him in delivering his verbal message. An example of this is when you use your hand to describe the size or the shape of something. Sometimes, they are used to emphasize a point. Think of your speech as written words and of illustrators as punctuation marks.

Have you ever observed someone talking on the phone and making hand gestures even though the person on the other end couldn't see it? This is because illustrators come almost automatically to a person. Compared to the other types of emblems, illustrators occur more naturally to people and they tend to be used more often.

A person who uses gestures too much and too often sends off the idea that he is impulsive. Likewise, a person who rarely uses gesticulations may come across as distant and impersonal. It could imply that they do not care that much to be in the conversation. The frequency in which a person uses gesticulation may help you gauge their social status. People in authoritative positions are less likely to use gestures except for a few deliberate movements.

Metaphoric Gestures

People use these types of gestures to provide a visual representation of complex concepts.

Affect displays

These refer to gestures that are used to convey the speaker's emotion. It may be as simple as holding the body in a protective manner to express anxiety.

Regulators

Regulators are often combinations of eye contact, facial expressions, hand gestures, head gestures, and vocal cues. People use them to create better control or understanding in a conversation. An example of this is when a person drops his arms after he has made his point.

Beat Gestures

Have you ever seen someone create rhythmic beating movements with his hand while speaking? It can be brief-- a single beat used by the speaker to capture your attention and place emphasis on an important point.

Chapter 9: Common Hand Gestures and What They Mean

The Precision Grip

Have you ever seen a person hold his index finger with his thumb to make a small circle while talking to you? This means that he's trying to persuade you. The Precision Grip is a hand gesture that is often used by politicians. They use this to create a point when they are making a speech. It gives off the idea that the speaker has chosen his words very carefully. Compared to pointing with an index finger, people tend to find this gesture less aggressive and politicians know it.

Pointing

A person often uses the index finger to communicate the presence of danger, to direct others, or to show a point of interest. However, this is often perceived as dominating, especially when the index finger has been replaced by the thumb. Sometimes, you may notice a speaker pointing with the use of an object—a pen, a ruler, etc.—instead of his finger. That's because speakers understand that by using a tool, they influence the listener into thinking that they are more efficient.

Finger Waving

Depending on the context, the person may be waving his finger in a scolding, authoritative manner. If it is done playfully, the intent may either be flirtatious or humorous.

Hand to the Chest

When a person places his palm to his chest, he does this to express the sincerity of his emotions. He may be trying to show that he is taking full responsibility of something. Sometimes, people do this to express the depth of their gratitude. This hand gesture is also often used when apologizing.

Hand Rubbing

Have you ever noticed a person rubbing his hands while he's speaking to you? Depending on the speed of his hand rubbing, it could mean either one of two things. If he's rubbing his hands slowly, then this communicates expectations leading to self-gain. If you're involved, then this self-gain may probably be at your expense. On the other hand, if he is rubbing his hands excitedly, then this communicates positive expectation. He is anticipating a positive outcome that may benefit him or the both of you.

Sleeve Rolling

There is a reason why people often pull their sleeves up before a fight or before engaging in manual labor. If you see a person rolling his sleeves, this signifies readiness or confidence and reveals an assertive trait. This may also be used as a means to intimidate.

Fist Shaking

Ever had someone shake their fists at you? Consider this as power play. It is an attempt to show their decisiveness. It may be that the speaker is trying to intimidate you or is trying to inspire you to perform aggressive action.

The Steeple

When a person holds the tips of his fingers together, this means that he is expressing his power or control. This can be viewed as confidence. Sometimes, it can be seen as arrogance. You'll often see this done by authoritative figures such as managers and doctors.

Attraction and Hand Gestures

Hand gestures are often used by people to signify attraction. If someone is attracted to you, they may perform a few unconscious hand movements that tend to encourage physical intimacy. This is done more often by females to create an impression of innocence and vulnerability and thus, appealing to the male's protective instincts. Examples of this are touching and drawing attention to the legs, exposing and touching one's neck, and touching the face especially the lips.

Preening

Preening actions may also signify attraction if they are done to draw attention towards an attractive part of a person. Similarly, it can be a reaction to something negative. For example, when people find someone attractive, they almost automatically straighten up, adjust their clothing, or flick their hair. Also, when experiencing a distasteful event, preening is used to provide the individual with a momentary means of distraction.

Deceit and Hand Gestures

Watching a person's hand gestures is a means of determining whether he is trying to deceive you. This doesn't necessarily mean that he is lying. It may be that he is uncertain about the information that he is trying to relay or that he is exaggerating a certain fact.

- When a person touches his mouth while he is speaking to you, he is unconsciously creating a barrier. In a way, he is unintentionally attempting to prevent himself from telling a lie.

- Likewise, if a person pulls on his earlobe while delivering a message, he is unconsciously trying to shield his ears from hearing untruthful statements.

- Remember Pinocchio? While a person's nose might not literally grow longer when he lies, it does tend to itch. When you notice that a person is touching his nose while he is talking to you, be alert.

- In some instances, rubbing one's eyes is a person's way of avoiding eye contact.

- Rubbing one's forehead or one's temple is another pacifying behavior designed to comfort a person while telling something less than truthful.

- Keep in mind that in the presence of a real itch, the scratches tend to appear more deliberate whereas scratching done to relieve psychological tension tends to be brief and light.

Tension and Hand Gestures

In the face of fear, the body's immediate response is to freeze, to fight, or to flee. As a result, the muscles tense up and build energy. However, in circumstances where this energy cannot be employed on a particular purpose, it is used to perform some futile activities such as touching the face, etc.

- Whenever people hear bad news, one of the most common reactions is covering the mouth with the hand.

- If a person fully or partially covers his face, it signifies feelings of embarrassment, either for himself or for others.

- If a person slaps his forehead, this can be construed as a self-punishing behavior. This is why a lot of people tend to slap themselves on the forehead whenever they forget something.

- If you ask a person a question and you notice him touch his mouth when he answers, this could mean that he is uneasy about answering your question. This means that you'll have to be cautious about believing in his answer.

Chapter 10: Head Gestures

The head is the sensory center of the human body. This is why it tends to move away from the things that you perceive as a threat. Likewise, the head has a tendency to move towards the things that it likes. Instinctively, you understand that when a person nods, he means yes and when a person shakes his head, he means to say no. But the truth is, there's so much more to the head nod and the head shake. Head gestures may be used to indicate whether or not a person agrees with what you are saying or whether or not their thoughts are compatible with yours. It can also be used to gauge their level of commitment to a conversation or an event. Head gestures are a means of detecting where a person's attention lies. More than that, head movement can be used as a means of controlling a conversation.

Reminders:

You'll be able to determine if one understands or agrees with you if he nods his head vigorously or rhythmically.

Meanwhile, if a person shakes his head slowly, it signifies his disbelief. If he, however, shakes his head faster, then this indicates that he is decisively disagreeing with what you are saying.

Head movements that are inconsistent, especially with eyes glancing to the sides, reveal that one is in a state of discomfort. He may be looking for an escape from the conversation.

When a person is angry, he tends to thrust his head forward. Likewise, when he is afraid, he has the tendency to retreat the head. The reason for this is when one feels threatened his initial response is to protect the head. And when a person is provoked, the common instinct to protect the head is suppressed momentarily.

A tilted head can mean several things depending on the circumstance. If you are conversing with someone, a head tilt followed by a nod means that he perceives your information as relevant and that you may proceed. This is particularly useful during interviews.

If one tilts his head upward and to his side, it means that he is surprised.

If a head tilt is accompanied by a brief glance to the side, this could mean that a person is trying to evaluate something; even more so if he is stroking his chin or touching his cheek.

Mirroring

Have you ever noticed that people who are related or have spent plenty of time with each other reflect similarities in their gestures and attitudes? Some friends, for instance, tend to subconsciously imitate each other's speech patterns. This is called Mirroring. The nodding of one's head, for example, implies synchronicity of thoughts between individuals. If the person you are conversing with produces no head movement at all, it's either they don't understand what you are saying or they don't agree with it or don't like it. In fact, sometimes, when speakers notice that the listeners' heads remain very still, they have a tendency to nod their heads in order to encourage the listeners to do the same. Keep this in mind when someone starts nodding at you persuasively.

The Nod

There are times when a nod is really more than just a nod. Studying the rhythm and the length of a head nod can help you identify its meaning.

- If a nod is slow and drawn-out, it means that the listener agrees with you and is encouraging you to keep talking. It's an assurance that he is all-ears and that you should take your time.

- On the other hand, a small nod accompanied by a smile means that the listener is attempting to connect with you and to encourage you.

- When a nod, however, is rapid and when a person is touching his ear, this means that he is starting to grow impatient. Chances are he already got your point. It's either he's urging you to move on to the next topic or he's waiting for an opportunity to voice his opinion on the matter.

- When the listener, though, is nodding while focusing his eyes in another direction, this means that he is either uninterested or distracted. As mentioned, the head has a propensity to move towards things that it deems more pleasant.

- On the other hand, this may mean that he is still busy processing any information that you shared earlier. In this case, give him time to absorb your words or make an effort to clarify their meanings.

- Head movements are also used to show recognition. When the head nod is used as a formal way of greeting someone, this implies that the person would like to maintain his distance. This often occurs between employers and employees and in times when a handshake or any form of physical contact is deemed less than appropriate. It could also mean that the person is trying not to look overly interested.

The Shake

While shaking the head is a universally accepted means of showing that one disagrees with another's point, it is now rarely used by people on purpose. This is because in most cultures, shaking the head from side to side while another person is still speaking may be considered as an act of rudeness. However, no matter how a person tries to control his head movements, his negative thought may still manifest itself through other unconscious head gestures, even one as subtle as the cut-off gesture.

A No without a Head Shake:

- Do you notice how when you disagree with someone or when you are distressed by a particular scenario, you tend to turn your body away? You may turn your back on something or just turn your head away from it. As a rule, the more severe your negative reaction is, the more of your body you tend to move away. The more you dislike something or the idea or something, the more unlikely you are to engage in it.

- Gestures that reflect impatience on the part of the listener may be seen as continuous tapping movements, glancing to the sides, and uttering empty remarks.

- Keep in mind though that similar to distracted head nodding, a faraway glance may also mean that a person is still trying to digest earlier information. In such cases, allow them to process the information before advancing towards a new topic.

- Sometimes, before deciding on the meaning of a head shake or a head nod, it is necessary to have a clue about one's cultural background. Keep in mind that in some places, like in the Balkan regions, a head nod means no and head shake means yes.

Chapter 11: The Eyes

From the Latin *oculus*, Oculesics refers to the study of the eyes as used in nonverbal communication. There's a reason why a person's peepers is considered as a window to his soul. For one thing, it's the only part of his body language that he can have no absolute control over. While hand gestures and even head gestures can be faked, even the most expert speaker will have a hard time controlling the dilation and the contraction of his pupils. Whenever you speak to someone about something that captures their fancy, you will notice their pupils dilating. Likewise, when you immediately switch the topic to something that doesn't interest them, you will see their pupils contract.

Have you ever had a thought that a particular person's eyes "look evil"? Or perhaps you've encountered the term "hungry eyes". That's because eye behavior has long been associated with people's personalities. We all seem to have an inherent ability to understand what a person is saying simply by looking at his eyes. For example, children don't need their parents to tell them to be quiet. Sometimes, a look is enough.

Eye Contact and Lying

While it may be true that lack of eye contact indicates that a person may be lying, too much eye contact can also mean that they are trying to deceive you. It is a sign of over-awareness. Keep in mind that persistent eye contact may be perceived as a threat and in some cultures, they are considered as rude. Studies show that staring too long into the eyes of an animal is likely to get a person into trouble because the animal feels threated by the stare.

On the other hand, avoiding eye contact is an indication of a person's shame over his dishonesty. As mentioned earlier, when you see the listener looking away, you should also consider the possibility that he is merely trying to contemplate over the previously received information. Ultimately, the best indicator of genuine interest and truthfulness is regular intervals of eye contact.

Attraction and Blinking

Humans have an unconscious need to blink. However, the frequency may be altered when a person's emotions become affected by the person he is conversing with. If you notice a person blinking more than six to ten times every minute while speaking with you, there is a chance that they are attracted to you. Also, blinking can be used by an individual as a way of controlling the movements of his eyes. One may blink frequently to conceal his excitement.

Eye Direction

Observing the direction of a person's eyes can help give you a clue about the nature of his thoughts. For example, if a person's eyes look towards his left, this means that he is attempting to remember something. Alternately, if a person's eyes move towards his right, his thoughts at the present are more creative in nature. In other words, he may be trying to conjure up something through his imagination. This may mean that he is being deceitful. It is important to note, however, that it is possible for these indicators to be reversed in cases of left-handed individuals. When a person looks sideways to his right, this means that he is trying to imagine sounds. When a person looks downward and to the right, he is accessing his emotions. When he is looking downward to the left, this is an indication that he is rationalizing.

Chapter 12: Reading The Face

Facial Expressions

Think of your face as a projector. It reflects both your feelings and intentions towards other people. Controlling one's facial expression is possible through it may be challenging as it involves an inner struggle. There are several things to remember when understanding a person through his facial expression.

Remember that genuine emotions don't last very long on a person's face.

Sometimes, real emotions are barely visible. When the expression on a person's face appears to be too pronounced, there's a high chance that he is faking it. A fake expression is naturally exaggerated since one is trying to convince people that he is feeling a certain way.

Eyebrows also say a lot. Sometimes, when a person recognizes you, his eyebrows raise instantly. Depending on the context, a person's raised eyebrows could also mean that he is expressing doubt or skepticism or that he is attempting to challenge your authority.

The Mouth

You can also say a lot about a person through the movements of his mouth. A smile, for example, is one of the most significant parts of facial body language. As a universal rule, smiles are more genuine when they are symmetrical and they reach the eyes. Fake smiles, on the other hand, remain only on a person's mouth.

- When you see a person with a pasted smile, this usually suggests that they are trying to suppress their irritation. A tight-lipped smile, on the other hand, can mean that the person is trying to hide a secret. This signifies dislike or lack of trust. It can also signal an impending rejection.
- A twisted smile is indicative of sarcasm. When a person smiles and his jaw appears to be dropped lower compared to that of a spontaneous smile, this means that the smile has been practiced and is likely to be fake. To know when a person is teasing, observe whether his head is tilted sideways and downward as he smiles.
- If one's bottom lip is jutting outward, this means that he is upset about something. He may be trying to gain your sympathy or he may be genuinely saddened.
- A pursed mouth could also mean that a person is upset. However, in some cases, it also shows pensiveness or impatience.
- If you notice a person poking his tongue out briefly, as though he had just tasted something repulsive, this is a sign of disapproval.
- People who laugh naturally show that they are at ease. To identify genuine laughter, see if it spreads throughout the entire upper body of a person. A forced laughter is an effort to drive away tension. This reflects nervousness. Another outward sign of inner tension is when a person bites his lip.
- When a person grinds his teeth, it is a visible sign of either stress or suppression of emotions. The same goes with chewing gum.

- Individuals sometimes use smoking or thumb-sucking as a means of comforting themselves. The same goes with chewing on a pen. So when you see someone doing this, he is probably experiencing stress.
- Nail-biting is another external display of stress. It is a self-comforting behavior that indicates an individual's frustration.

Chapter 13: Proxemics, Posture, and Body Movements

Proxemics

Remember your school days when you or your classmates would choose to sit at the back if you find the subject boring and in front if you find the subject interesting? This is proof that a person's preferred distance to something or someone holds much meaning. Proxemics as a study concerns itself with how people treat their personal space, their proximity with others and the amount of distance in which they feel most comfortable.

- A distance of 0-6 inches is referred to as Close Intimate space. This suggests that the person is in a familiar relationship where physical touching is allowed. This is common among lovers.

- A space of 6-18 inches is referred to as Intimate. This commonly occurs between close friends and relations. In some cases, such as visiting crowded places and playing contact sports, people consent to this degree of proximity. Otherwise, if a person is this close to you needlessly, it may be perceived as a threatening gesture or an act of intrusion.

- The Personal zone is a distance of 18 inches to 4 feet. This is usually observed among family and close friends. Touching is allowed but intimacy is considered uncomfortable.

- A distance of 4-12 feet is called a Social-Consultative zone which is common in business interactions and in non-touch social activities. An individual who keeps this kind of distance from you is likely to consider a handshake as the only acceptable means of touching.

- A distance of 12 feet and beyond is considered as a Public zonal space. This means no interaction. Individuals who establish this kind of space means that they are attempting to avoid interaction with others.

Posture

Observing a person's posture can tell you something about his personality. It can tell you whether a person is the submissive type or the dominant type. It can tell you whether an individual is alert and focused or whether his thoughts are someplace else. For example, if you see a person sitting with his body bent forward, it suggests that he is bored.

- If a person is in a position where the trunk is exposed, this is considered as an Open posture. This is normally indicative of friendliness, honesty, and enthusiasm.

- If a person's posture is geared towards concealing his body, this is called a Closed posture. A closed posture suggests that he is hostile, anxious, or indifferent towards you.

Arm Movements

Crossed arms or arms enfolded over the chest suggest either defensiveness or lack of willingness. In this case, the arms signify a protective barrier between you and the person. In some cases though, people cross their arms when they are feeling cold so be careful about jumping into conclusions.

- Crossed arms accompanied by clenched fists are a defensive gesture that signifies strong feelings of hostility. The clenching of one's fist may be interpreted as obstinacy or indifference towards another's feelings.

- If you see a person gripping his own upper arms, this suggests that he has feelings of insecurity. He may be feeling sad or unsafe.

- If a woman's arm is draped across her body and she is grasping her other arm, this means that she is nervous.

- Authority is often expressed by a person who is holding his arms behind his back with his hands clasped together. You will observe this in teachers and policemen. This gesture also suggests confidence.

- Scratching one's shoulder or adjusting one's clothing with the arm across the body is a means of forming a protective barrier. Therefore, this shows nervousness. Another way to spot apprehension in men is when they are attempting to cover their genital regions with either their hands or their arms. Another typically male protective gesture is holding papers across one's chest. Likewise, when a woman's handbag is held in front of her body, this shows that she is either worried or scared.

Leg Movements

- You will notice in a seated person that their knees tend to point towards something that catches their attention. If they are pointed towards you, then it is a sign or attentiveness. At the same time, a person's legs have a tendency to point away from anything that is deemed unexciting. Similarly, when in a standing position, one's foot may point towards the direction of interest.

- Uncrossed legs generally show an open attitude. Likewise, crossed legs are indicative of a closed attitude or hesitation.

- If a woman is sitting in a manner wherein the legs are parallel to each other, this indicates a sense of propriety.

- When a man's legs are open while sitting, this suggests either arrogance or aggressiveness. Open-crotch postures in males create a sexual suggestion.

- Locked ankles while sitting may mean defensiveness. On the other hand, when a person stands in a scissor stance, this may mean submissiveness.

- When one's knees buckles while he is standing, chances are he is under pressure. This is due to the thought of carrying a heavy burden.

- Shoe play by a female shows that she is attempting to flirt. It may also suggest that she is simply in a relaxed mood.

Interpreting Handshakes

¬ When another person's handshake is vigorous, this shows energy. He feels enthusiastic about meeting with you. This is why you'll notice this kind of handshake done by many evangelists and other motivational speakers.

¬ Contrary to popular opinion, a weak handshake does not necessarily suggest weakness in a person. A person may simply be strong yet passive. In fact, creative people such as musicians and artists tend to have gentler handshakes. On the other hand, those who aren't accustomed to handshaking tend to have more feeble handshakes.

¬ If someone shakes your hand with his palm facing downward, this portrays dominance. Similarly, if someone shakes your hand with his palm facing upwards, this shows that his behavior towards you is accommodating.

¬ If a person shakes with both hands, they may be trying to portray trustworthiness, whether it is genuine or not.

¬ A vertical handshake suggests equality. It is a non-threatening gesture and sends the message that one seeks neither to dominate nor to submit.

¬ A handshake that is firm is meant to imply confidence, whether it is real or feigned. One misconception is that a firm handshake automatically means that a person has a solid character.

¬ When a person shakes your hand and then clasps your right arm, it means that they are either seeking control or expressing paternal emotions towards you. This type of handshake may be construed as somewhat condescending.

Chapter 14: Four Simple Personality Exercises

Exercise 1 - Pay Attention To The Four C's

In order to read people, you have to follow a few basic guidelines known as the four C's. The four C's are:

- Read Concentratedly
- Observe Carefully
- Decide Confidently
- Practice Constantly

To begin with you must concentrate when attempting to read someone. This can be accomplished simply by paying attention with all your senses when you speak to someone or observe someone.

The next C stands for observing carefully. When you look at people, it's important not to jump to conclusions but to simply observe before making any kind of judgment.

The next two C's are all about deciding confidently and practicing constantly. Practice makes perfect because the more you follow these guidelines the easier it becomes to decide what category someone falls in.

Understanding people is one of the greatest weapons you possess. The more you use them, the better you will understand how they work.

Exercise 2 - Pay Attention to The Body Type

This is an important step to take. If someone has a round shaped body this would tell you they are The Alimentive Type or The Enjoyer. The Thoracic or the Thriller, on the other hand, has a high chest and they tend to be long-waisted. A woman might also have a wasp waist or a very thin waistline. A Thriller might also have what is known as a red face so if you see someone with a red face and a long waist, you know they are the Thriller.

The Muscular type or The Worker is obviously muscular and firm and this type of person is usually very solid in structure. The Osseous or The Stayer, on the other hand, has an overly developed bony framework, with prominent ankles, wrists, and knuckles.

Last but certainly least is the Thinker. The Cerebral or The Thinker is the brain of the group and the person who lives to meditate. The Cerebral is the opposite of the Enjoyer in the fact that they tend to be top heavy with a proportionally large head.

Now bear in mind these body types are for the pure unmixed person, so it's important to remember many people are combinations of different types.

Exercise 3 - Notice How They Move

This can be a fun thing to do and once you start noticing how people move, you will be able to easily pinpoint their type.

The Enjoyer is a man of unhurried movements. They tend to make as few moves as possible, because of their large structure. When this type walks, they might even appear to waddle. The Enjoyer might also appear to be round or circular.

The Thriller shows the slightest displeasure or surprise by the blood rushing to the face. This type also displays energetic movements, with a hair-trigger type of nimbleness.

The Worker, on the other hand, is built around the square, and his entire physique may be a combination of squares.

The Stayer has a boney appearance and may appear raw-boned. This type might also have large joints or angular hands and might appear firm, fixed or impassive as though everything about him is permanent.

The Thinker once again has a large head because of his tendency to be lost in thought. People that daydream a lot are classified as Thinkers.

Exercise Number 4 - Notice How They Feel About Food

Food can tell us a lot about someone. For example, some people forget to eat while others never ever miss a meal. The Enjoyer never forgets about dinner because they tend to really enjoy their food, just like they enjoy their life. The Enjoyer might also like to describe his food, by telling you what he had for breakfast or lunch.

The Thinker, on the other hand, is much more interested in food for the brain, as opposed to food for the body.

The Thinker might be perfectly happy to enjoy a snack with his book, where the Enjoyer would rather sit down to a large meal. The Thriller, on the other hand, tends to be fidgety and they may talk more than they eat.

The Worker, who tends to have a square head and jaw, may have a forceful walk or a loud voice and when this person sits, he does so with a definiteness and force.

The Stayer is very formal in their movements, so they may approach the table with that same formality. The Stayer doesn't like change either, so they may enjoy eating the same thing at every meal.

The Thinker may prefer lighter meals, because food tends to bog them down and take away from their brainpower.

Look for these simple things and you will be one step closer to being able to read someone's unique personality.

Exercise Number 5 - Notice Eye Signals

Noticing someone's eyes can tell you a lot about their character. When you speak to people, look directly into their eyes. If their eyes are shifting or darting around you can be sure that they are uncomfortable for some reason. Sincere and honest people tend to look directly into your eyes, in a loving manner.

When someone looks to the left, it usually means they are trying to remember something. On the other hand, if they look to the right, it is often said they are trying to make something up in their mind.

These two eye movements typically correspond to the region in the brain being accessed. To put it another way, when someone is looking up and to the left, they are usually remembering a picture or a moment in the past. If they happen to look up and to the right, they are usually trying to construct a picture in their mind, which is much different than remembering a picture.

If someone is looking down and to the right it is said they are accessing certain feelings.

Now it's important to keep in mind that different cultures have different rules so some people may not look directly into your eyes for cultural reasons.

Exercise Number 6 - Notice Someone's General Appearance

This should be done very subtly. Looking at someone's general overall appearance can give you valuable clues as to what kind of a day they are having. If someone looks disheveled, they are obviously having trouble coping with their day. If someone appears sloppily dressed, that might indicate they are suffering from depression.

While much of this is common sense, it does pay to look at the details. If someone is impeccably dressed that is a good sign that they enjoy taking care of themselves. On the other hand, if someone is dressed casually, it could mean they have a casual and playful approach to life.

When analyzing someone, pay attention to the little details like the condition of their shoes, their handbag or even their hair.

Exercise Number 7 - Asking and Listening

Communication is so important, because without it we don't have much left. Asking and listening is integral when it comes to understanding people. A casual conversation can reveal a lot about someone's character.

If someone is happy, you will know it as soon as you talk to them. Happy people are usually happy to engage in casual conversation. People that are unhappy or stressed out will have difficulty with a casual conversation because they will be focused more on their problems.

If you engage in a conversation and the person looks away or looks anxious, that is a good sign that they don't want to talk. If you talk to someone and they are happy to talk back, their body language will be open and available.

It is also very important to be a good listener because you can tell a lot about someone by merely listening and observing. The more they talk, the more will be revealed about their character.

The more you practice, the better you will be at reading people.

Chapter 15. The Fundamentals of Human Psychology and Manipulation, Persuasion and Deception

In this chapter you will learn:

Human Psychology and Manipulation, Persuasion and Deception
Ethical Considerations
How the Power of Suggestion Changes Perception
Using the Right Words in a Question
Statement by an Authority

Human Psychology and Manipulation, Persuasion and Deception

There are a lot of theories out there on the functions and tendencies of the human brain. There is also a lot of literature that discuss how people form their opinions, belief systems and behavior patterns. Conversely, there will be a lot of theories that will discuss how people generally behave in certain situations, contexts and environments. With all these theories and literature on the subject of human psychology, one thing is certain: In order to persuade, manipulate or deceive a person, you have to align your mind with their situation, context or environment. In other words, the first step in persuading, manipulating or deceiving someone is to fully understand their mindset.

How do you fully understand the mind of the other person? How do you use this understanding of the other person's mind in order to persuade, deceive or manipulate him into your way of thinking? The fundamental answer to this question is: find what drives and motivates the other person to take an action. As an illustrative case, does the other person do something for the money? Does he do it for glory? Does he do it for power? Does he do it for fame? Understand his psychology and his state of mind. Once you are armed with the other person's drive and motivations, it is now time to strategically position your conversations and requests in such a way that will be beneficial to him and his motivations. In this way, he will quickly accept your request with little to no resistance. Do you know why? This is because he will see you as being very much like him because of the way you controlled the conversation and made your request. As such, he will feel the innate compulsion to comply with your request. This is the fundamental tenet of persuasion, deception and manipulation.

The major theme of this work is to persuade, manipulate and deceive the other person without the other person knowing or noticing it. In other words, your goal is to keep your efforts and intentions hidden and concealed from your target. Therefore, the strategies and techniques that you will learn in Chapters 2, 3 and 4 are specifically designed to help you bypass the human mind's critical factor (persuasion, manipulation and deception) without the process being known to the receiver. As such, your goal is to accomplish your intentions without significant resistance or reaction by your target person or group of people.

The Logic Falls, But the Emotions Win

If you ever studied the rules of logic, you would see that manipulating, deceiving, or persuading a person may put you in this rather absurd situation, which is that of committing a fallacy. Fallacies, in themselves, are absurdities, meaning that your argument cannot possibly be held always true because it defies specific rules.

If you want your argument to be always valid and you want to influence the mind of others through the most logical means, then you may find that psychology is actually riddled with a lot of fallacies. There are the *argumentum ad baculum, argumentum as edacitam, argumentum ad verecundiam,* and a lot of other Latin terms for false appeals. People commit these fallacies because they are appealing to emotions, authority, or turn of events that they, of course, cannot possibly predict.

However, this is the good part about the real world – not all people are convinced that everything that falls under good logic is actually "sound" argument. A sound argument means that there are truths in this world that actually defy the laws of logic. However, their defiance of the law (as people can see it) makes the world a lot more real. There are times that people try to predict the weather, which of course is largely unpredictable. There are predictions that nail it, and there are those that would turn out in an unpredictable nature.

While there are some books that would make you think that the right path to influencing people is to play with their heads according to the laws of logic, this book will teach you how to greatly influence others by putting yourself in their shoes. This is all about empathizing with others, and then putting a believable and sound argument in their head that will work well to your benefit. That is because in the real world, people are more likely to react according to what they feel and not according to what the truth in their heads says. You have probably observed how many people have eaten ice cream "just because." They would not argue that a hormone told them to do it, and it is because of the firing of neurons in their head. They eat ice cream because they believe that they are just happy to do it. Now, you will influence people to act according to your plan just how they like their ice cream – they will be just happy to do what you ask them to do.

Ethical Considerations

There are a lot of reasons why a certain person may want to manipulate, deceive and persuade another person. Now, the question is: Is it ethical to manipulate, deceive and persuade another person into your way of thinking? The answer really depends on you. No one can determine whether what you are doing is ethical or not but you. However, there are a lot of instances in society where you need to perform some specific techniques in manipulation, deception and persuasion in order to advance your position.

As an illustrative example in the international political arena, let us suppose you are the President of the United States and Russia is trying to engage you in a nuclear arms race. Of course, you do not want to engage in another World War. Therefore, your target person is the Russian leader and your intention or position is to stop any world conflict and maintain peace. In this case, it would be very useful to utilize techniques on persuasion, deception and manipulation in order to advance your position of world peace and harmony.

If you are in the field of business, your target persons, of course, are your clients and customers. In addition, your intention is to make them buy your products or avail your services.

If you are an environmental lawyer, your target persons are policymakers, lobbyists and the public. In addition, your intention is to persuade them to join your cause in protecting the environment.

When you look at the topic of mind control closely, it is practically a game of persuasion, which is arguably played every day. It would be, of course, up to you to think of the purpose why you would want to learn these tricks. As

Machiavelli would say, everything becomes a means to a specific end. The art of mind manipulation, however, does not mean that you are denying your targets the use of free will. Instead, you are giving them something that they are most likely looking for – a sense of compelling choice, which serves as guidance for their behavior.

At the end of the day, it is the extent of your actions and your personal belief system that will determine whether the tactics and strategies that you use are ethical or not.

The Power of Suggestion Changes Perception

Remember that the major goal of this book is to create a specific change in the thinking of your target person without that person being aware of the changes in his or her thinking. If you are a businessman, your target audience is your customers and your position or intention is to make them buy your products or avail your services.

In this regard, one of the most effective ways in making a change in the way of thinking of your customers (or your target) is to change the way you speak. In other words, you have to make use of the right words to make your customers desire what you are offering. If you are watching commercial advertisements in the television and also on YouTube right now, you will realize short commercial videos are enticing because they address the specific problems of their target persons using the words (or lingo) of the latter. Therefore, there is an emotional feeling that the makers of the product or service fully understand your point of view, situation or environment just by the language used.

Now, when you think about the way commercials appear on TV, they are all offering two types of sensation – pleasure and pain. Essentially, they are playing on the two sensations that changed the course of humanity forever. Philosophers, religious orders, and tyrants all played with the concept of sensations with a similar belief that all people would want to do anything in order for them to obtain pleasure or to avoid pain. Thousands of years later, people still behave in the same premise. That is why the art of manipulation and mind control is still in business. You use our product, you avoid tooth decay is a typical example.

With that in mind, how do you think people prefer their brand of coffee over others? It is still the play of pleasure vs. pain. Some would believe that they prefer double shots of espresso in order for them to experience that pleasurable sensation of becoming awake much quicker, because they are annoyed with slowness. They want to reach the bitter taste of coffee as soon as they take a sip. However, they are in contrast with the latte people – they prefer milk over coffee, and they want to feel the caffeine like it is, in the form of slow waves in their bloodstream. Each will appeal to a different set of people, playing upon their needs.

However, try saying to an espresso lover that he can absorb more caffeine in a tall glass of latte than drinking 3 tall glasses of cappuccino. More often than not, that espresso lover would try switching to latte the next morning, because he is more likely to get what he wants quickly that way. At the end of this argument, people are not mostly concerned about the way they are getting what they want – they just want a method that would lead them closer to their goals in a quicker manner. They would like to think that their preferred methods are all shortcuts to a pleasurable experience.

With that in mind, it is rather easy for people to change their belief systems if the change is going to guarantee success. That is why there are just too many commercially available products of the same variant out there. Just imagine the number of toothpaste brands. However, spread the word that one brand would probably make a person's teeth fall off when he's in his 80s– it is almost guaranteed that people that are diehard fans of that brand would switch, or do a really strict scrutiny of their use of that product.

For this reason, when you are trying to learn to influence the minds of people around you, always try to understand how they truly feel about a product and what it does for them. One way or another, they buy a product because they believe that they want it. But once someone offers the idea that they should not want it anymore because it will cause them harm, they will reject that product. However, perhaps 7 out of 10 times, they would rather look for a similar product than quit using it daily. If you can offer cigarettes that would not give cancer and mouth problems yet offer the same satisfying drag as other brands, then you are almost guaranteed to be rich. People don't want cancer but they still want their cigarettes.

Why is that the case? It is because humans all desire what they are used to having. Now change that perspective and offer a benefit, or offer something that would improve their lives the easy way. Offer something that if they refused to take, they will put their lives at risk. The art of mind control is similar – the subconscious would always tell targets that they are moving towards pleasure and avoidance of pain.

Using the Right Words in a Question

The truth is, you can also use the right words in forming a question that will manipulate, deceive and persuade your target. For example, there was a psychological and behavioral experiment conducted by one of the leading scientists in the field of memory, Elizabeth Loftus, in the

1970s. In this experiment, she made people in a room view images of an accident between an automobile and a pedestrian. In the said images, the automobile (a red Datsun car) was shown together with a yellow Yield sign (traffic light) at the scene of the accident. After some time, she asked the group of people, “Did you see the Stop sign (red traffic light) together with the red Datsun car (the automobile involved in the accident?” The funny thing is, most of the people answered yes. Of course the correct answer must be in the negative because the sign was a yellow yield sign. The implication of this experiment is that if you use the right words in forming your question in such a way as to verbalize the information that you want to be altered, the memory of those listening is altered in your favor.

The trick is that people, more often than not, refer to association. The good thing is that the human language is so diverse that a word in a sentence, even though it may be a synonym, can actually change the entire context that the person is reacting upon. When you think about it, a sentence can mean the same thing but still generate different responses.

For example, you can ask a person about the importance of his role as a citizen during election time, with the hopes that you can get him to vote. You may ask two different, yet very similar questions: “Do you know how important it is that you vote?” or “Do you know your importance as a voter?” Note that you merely want that person to think about his duty as a citizen, which is to elect officials. However, a person who is asked the second question is more likely to be affected by the topic at hand. That is because you made sure that he is going to answer a question that is more appealing for him. You made him an important character in that story that you are trying to paint.

The right words in a question also involve senses that are more appealing to a person. You know that there are people who are more likely to decide according to what they see, and there are others who are more affected by the sound of the product. If you are trying to sell a guitar, a visual person would probably buy according to what he already saw on the stand, and there is no point in making him test it out for the sound – he is already "sold" the moment he saw it. An aural person, on the other hand, is more likely to buy from you if you ask him if he wants that guitar on the shelf that gives a rich, full, and bright sound. Note that you are offering the same product, but you are asking about the senses that appeal to that particular person more.

Statement by an Authority

Another fundamental principle in order to manipulate, deceive and persuade a target person is the 'statement by an authority' strategy. This means that a mere suggestion or statement by an authority figure can often modify and alter a person's visual memory in such a manner as to create a different memory that is favorable to the authority figure. The implication of this principle is that depending on the person who is doing the telling (is he an authority figure or is he another common person?), people will think different things about his suggestion or statement. Always remember that the authority figure differs from person to person. As an illustrative example, some people will consider a university professor as an authority figure while some people will consider a person who learned from hard-knocks as an authority figure. In other words, you have to put yourself in a situation where you will know the considered authority figure of your target person.

Now, suppose that you want to go to Las Vegas together with your friend. You have the knowledge that this friend considers Professor Smith from his Economics class as his authority figure. In this case you can say to your friend that, "I know how much you like Professor Smith from the university. Well, he said these things about going to Las Vegas . . ." See the magic that happens the minute the individual knows that his authority figure approves.

You might think that there are people who do not believe in authority. Well, you're right, so this cannot be a universal strategy to influence people. However, if you look at the history of this civilization, people have always rooted for any form of organization. People have always been on the lookout for someone who will provide them the information that they need to improve their lives, or someone they can look up to as an inspiration. While people may think that they can ignore and dismiss the importance of the government, they will still look for a leader.

To be able to influence a person, you must have either the qualities of a leader, or have your words come from someone influential. That way, those listening to the words you say wouldn't doubt you. You can see this all the time when people who are admired sponsor items for sale.

Chapter 16. Assuming the Role of the Controller

When you look at master mentalists that have the ability to control another person's will, or heavily influence decisions, you may think that they have superpowers. However, that power has also been the trick used by the greatest salesmen, politicians, lawyers, private investigators and even con men since time began. The art of bending another person's mind has been used for centuries, and that has ushered many civilizations to either flourish or become devastated.

So, what does it take to be able to be great at persuading, manipulating, or deceiving people? It does not take much – all you need to do is to assume the best asset of these mentalists, and that is self-esteem. For starters, that is what you would need to have in order to be convincing.

Why be Confident?

Being a good mentalist requires a tremendous success rate, because it would be very difficult to get out of a situation in the case of failure. Imagine the amount of explaining that you would have to do whenever you fail to deceive someone.

At the same time, people who are confident are the ones who can easily think of several strategies at once on how they can be successful. They are also the ones who have the passion to succeed and change their strategies if needed. Now, since influencing the minds of others requires a lot of psychological work, it would definitely be wise to become a person who can handle the pressure.

The thing about being confident is that you can be unfazed in front of your targets. You can calmly look at them in the eye with only one thing in your mind –your success. Since your mind is clear and you are able to make plans spontaneously based on another person's actions, you are able to make sure that you can give the right responses.

That is why poker players and street magicians have the ability to tell people what they need to by ensuring that their audience is bound to see something entertaining. But if they manage to break eye contact, break a sweat, or unknowingly give away their trick, all those people who are watching them are going to predict what they are going to do. Hence, the trick that they are preparing is bound to fail.

The art of mind control works similarly to that, the only difference is that you are trying to get so much more from another person. You are not merely trying to get their chips or their applause; you are trying to win their trust. Now, imagine what would happen if you were trying to sell an idea and you couldn't even manage to look the other person in the eye. Imagine what would happen if you were overly conscious about how you dress or you obviously wonder what other people are thinking about you, then you would not be able to secure what you want from other people in the first place. Your own insecurity would stop you in your tracks.

Become Credible

Credibility makes a good part of the game. You are more likely to influence people who are not going to put up defenses around you because it is apparent that you are trying to sell them something or use them according to your will. Now, while that may be your objective in order to achieve a much bigger goal, no person in this planet would be willing to do you a favor without his or her own interests in mind.

At this point, you have to keep in mind that you are not merely trying to plant an idea in your targets' mind, but also see to it that they see the benefit of this particular action. You need to provide them the idea that they can find comfort in your company, and that you are willing to show them the tricks that you have up your sleeves that will make things easier for them.

Credibility is not merely about becoming believable when it comes to the role that you are trying to assume. It is about the impression that you are someone important – a force to be reckoned with. You have to become a person that people would want to listen to.

Give Orders

Derren Brown, a world-famous mentalist, once showed his trick on how he can possibly predict what another person is going to choose to do. He was even able to predict what top advertising partners are going to come up with in a surprise task. However, he is also known for being a master of misdirection and influencing the subliminal mind. For that, he is known to provide the best orders when it comes to manipulating the mind.

A good mind controller knows how to deeply influence a person by manipulating the subliminal mind. That works by making use of everything that is around the target to plant an idea. For that reason, you are able to make sure that your environment is the best tool that you can use in order for you to influence others. The reason for that is that most people move according to what the environment dictates.

That is perhaps one of the best-kept secrets of mentalists. They instill their credibility on you by making sure that you are aware that they can carefully read your body language. However, they are merely reading what you would most possibly do according to the environment around you. For example, you are most likely to think of a 3-of-diamonds card when you see something that is similar to that around you. You may see that on the magician's shirt, or randomly placed inside the room that you are in.

For that reason, the best magicians and salesmen use this trick – they deliberately give orders to their target that would definitely imprint an idea in their mind. They manage to ask their target to use all the information that they can also observe in the environment, in order to provide their target the idea that everything is a spontaneous act. By providing the right type of orders, they manage to misdirect the target. Then what appears to their target is a pure trick.

However, you may not have to go through the entire staging, unless you are gunning for deception. You can always influence people without having to hide it.

Chapter 17. The 4 Golden Tactics for Manipulation

In this chapter you will learn:

Manipulation Tactic #1: Rapidly Build Rapport with Your Target
Manipulation Tactic #2: Use Content to Build Rapport with Your Target
Manipulation Tactic#3: Use Processes to Build Rapport with Your Target
Manipulation Tactic #4: Induce Reciprocity

Understanding Manipulation

What are you trying to do exactly? When you are trying to manipulate someone, you are deliberately forcing someone into doing things that would benefit you. Learning manipulation is among the toughest skills to learn in this lifetime for some, because of the amount of effort that is needed in order to make tactics work. However, there are some people who seem to be able to manipulate people instantly the moment they walk into a room. That skill, obviously, is not something that you can learn overnight.

Manipulation is a technique that requires you to make your target go in the direction that you want through the use of several, sequential tricks that have to be carefully timed. Manipulation techniques are also described as aggressive, meaning that all tactics that you use are designed to forcefully make your targets agree with your line of thinking, and doing so would require you to carefully observe your target in order to see the right sets of tactics that would work on them. In many occasions, you will never get enough opportunity to get to know your target well in order to actually test how your tricks would work on them.

In order for you to move closer to your targets and make sure that you would be able to wear down their defenses until they are vulnerable, make sure that you use the following manipulation tactics. Not only would they allow you to move closer to your chosen targets, you would also ensure that you can create a comprehensive series of techniques that would allow you to manipulate them when you encounter them again.

Manipulation Tactic # 1: Rapidly Build Rapport with Your Target

According to the dictionary, rapport is a relationship of emotional affinity or mutual trust. To put it simply, rapport with the other person simply means that your feelings and emotions are strategically in sync or in harmony with theirs. As a rule, a person will feel a good amount of rapport with another person if the former likes the latter. Therefore, building rapport with your target person will be one of the most important tools that you can use in order to manipulate them.

Now, what is the valuable test in order to determine if you have a good amount of rapport with another person? The test is this: Does this person respond to my actions, thoughts and words in a manner that is positive? If the answer is yes, you have successfully built rapport without you knowing it. If the answer is no, you have to use some techniques and strategies to build a good amount of rapport with your target person. That means you need to do more work.

The following strategies are proved to facilitate building of rapport with another person:

Match and mirror the other person's body position:
Have a conversation where you will talk about subjects of common interest.

Why is mirroring interests and actions very important when trying to manipulate a target? That is because people are more likely to respond to you once that they recognize that you are in the same field. That is why a child is more likely to respond to an adult who would tend to sit down or kneel when talking to him. By physically insinuating that they are on the same level, the adult places the child on a fair level playing ground. The child then reciprocates by listening intently.

Communicative adults who are interested in other people are those who would tend to do the same. That is why they would also stoop their shoulders when they are talking to a slouched person, or keep their chest out when talking to a proud one. People who are used to building rapport with people are known to take on the posture and mannerisms of the person whom they are talking to.

As you go along the journey of practicing these skills, you will certainly be good at it. This means that your skills in rapport will flow subconsciously and naturally with your conversation with another person. In fact, there will be times that you are not even consciously aware that you already had built a good amount of rapport with that person. More advanced application of techniques on building a good amount of rapport are covered in the subsequent manipulation tactics.

Manipulation Tactic # 2: Use Content to Build Rapport with Your Target

Conduct a sort of study on your target person. For example, put yourself in positions where you will be able to learn about subjects that your target is interested in or is connected to emotionally.

If you are also interested in the subjects that your target is interested in, then your work in manipulating such a person will be relatively easy. Why is that? It is because people are more likely to respond positively when the person who is trying to engage them is similar to them. For example, if you are a billionaire who made his riches through software development, you are most likely to either like the other billionaires in the same room, or you are going to talk to others who develop their own software. Remember that people are more likely to talk to you if you exude a personality that they also exhibit.

On the other hand, if you are not interested in the subjects that your target is interested in, then your work in manipulating such person will be relatively more difficult. If this is the case, what you can do is to learn about these subjects by reading about them in the newspaper or by using Internet search engines for research. Remember that you do not need to have an expert knowledge of these subjects. Rather, having some basic knowledge about these subjects is enough to give you a head start in the conversation.

The reason for this is that people like to have conversations about subjects that they are truly interested in. Having conversations about these subjects lowers their mental defenses and *allows* in new data and information. In other words, once the mental defenses of your target are down, this is the perfect time to manipulate such target with your new data or information.

At the same time, keep in mind that people are mostly interested in themselves and if you are just like them, they are going to be interested in you. For that same reason, musicians hang out with musicians to have a musician talk. That is also the same reason why a fellow musician is more likely to sell a particular type of beer, than a person from a beer company would. That is because the former already knows how a musician can enjoy that drink, but a salesman from a beer company wouldn't be interested in that experience.

However, a musician is also more likely to buy beer from someone who is interested in music, or who is trying to learn an instrument. It is not because they really like the product – it's just that they genuinely like the seller. When you observe the real world, people are more likely to buy anything from a person who tries to empathize with their interests.

Manipulation Tactic # 3: Use Processes to Build Rapport with Your Target

Apart from building a rapport by having a conversation on a subject that your target is interested in, there is another strategy you can use that is also effective in manipulating your target. This strategy uses processes with the goal of making you appear similar with your target.

How do you execute this manipulation tactic? You can execute this by performing the same activity (processes) that your target is currently involved in. These processes include the following:

Place or setting for work
Type of work
Small and medium business or enterprises
Social structure
Family
Clubs
Sports
Communities
Hobbies
Affiliations (fraternity, masonry, politics, religion etc.)

As you can see, there are a lot of processes that you can use in order to build rapport with your target. Perhaps you have both worked in the military before and are thus both army veterans. Perhaps both of you are lawyers or surgeons by profession. Perhaps you are both members of a Toastmasters club. Perhaps you are both into fishing in the lakes. Perhaps you are both members of a fraternity or sorority. Now, once you have a process that gives you common ground with your target, you have to involve this common ground as a point of connection in your activities with your target. For example, if you are both into fishing in the lake, you can invite your target into fishing this weekend! This way, you will be able to demonstrate to your target that you are just like him or her through shared experience/s. In other words, the common ground is critical to your success in manipulating your target.

Now, when you think about it, you can convince a person to do something for you if you see to it that you empathize with the environment that he is in. If you are trying to ask a fisherman a favor, you are more likely to get it in his wharf, not on a golf course. Introduce the idea that you are interested in what he does for a living by mentioning points of interests in his home environment. Mention that your grandparents once did fishing for a living, and that is how they were able to raise your parents. Say that you have always wanted to do fishing so you can go back to your roots. What you would most probably get is this – a new skill, and that favor that you asked.

Manipulation Tactic # 4: Induce Reciprocity

Initially, people do not buy your ideas, your products, your political office candidates, your causes or your service. Rather, they buy you! As such, your first goal is for your target to like you as a person more than anything else. One technique you can do for your target to like you is to induce reciprocity.

To put it simply, inducing reciprocity means that you will give away an object, service or favor to your target. Take note however, that this object, service or favor must be perceived as valuable by your target. The reason for this strategy is by giving your target person a valuable object, service or favor, he or she will be compelled to do likewise by the feeling of gratitude towards you.

You do not only observe this type of friendly manipulation in politics, but also everywhere else in life. Generally, this works by making a person remember that he technically owes you a favor. It would work better if you have been able to meet before, and you are able to change his circumstances dramatically in his favor. When you do this, say something subtle, but to the effect of "you owe me." That person would always associate you with the occurrence of the favor, and whenever he sees you, he would be obliged to give you small favors.

Why does this work? Well, it works because the person who owes you a favor does not really objectify you as a literal debtor – since you managed to help him overcome a difficult time, he would always want to extend help. And the best thing is that you do not have to do something great or put yourself in danger – the moment another person recognizes that you went out of your way to help a person who is not your relative, they develop a certain bond with you.

Now, going "out of your way" deliberately for another person is of course, deliberate manipulation. Any person with a sense of dignity and honor would definitely want to repay you in any form of favor that you ask them, as long as they can afford it. The key to getting the most out of reciprocity is to make them feel that the favor that you are going to ask them would cost them practically nothing, but is one that can establish a mutual benefit. It would then appear that you are also doing them a favor by letting them help you.

What does this establish then? You have built a relationship that would put you as the Alpha. As long as you are able to establish that you are the one who can think of a good plan that would benefit both of you, he would be happy to extend help to you. This works since that other person thinks that he would be a great addition to your plan. He becomes aware that you would not be successful if you did not reach out for his help. That makes him aware that somehow you would also be indebted to him.

Chapter 18. The 5 Golden Tactics for Persuasion

In this chapter you will learn to:

Understand persuasion
Make the Damaging Admission
Share a Part of You with Your Target
Knock Their Socks Off
Be Precise

Understanding Persuasion

When you are trying to persuade someone, what are you really trying to do? Persuasion, in its very nature, is the skill that allows you influence your target into allowing a new belief into his system. You do that by making sure that the belief that you are instilling in your target would fit with the way he thinks. You also do that by challenging the authorities that he listens to and making him assume that you are the authority of the new belief that you want him to acquire.

There are many ways that you can engineer persuasion, and in this chapter you will learn 5 of them. You can even engineer your own tactics based on the character of your target, but you have to create them in such a way that you go back to what persuasion really is. At this point, you will begin to realize that persuasion is a very powerful tool, and most people who have been using this skill for almost any relationship that they are in believe that it is even the foundation of the other skills discussed in this book, which are manipulation and deception. Persuasion allows you to move in and drop the defenses of your target, by placing them in a situation wherein they would change their beliefs.

Beliefs are very powerful when it comes to creating what is comfortable for people, which in turn dictates what they would repeatedly do. They are not 100% correct, and they are malleable according to experience. Because they can change depending on one's experience of the world, it becomes possible for you, the controller, to challenge them and make your targets perceive their environment to be something else. It all sounds easy, but of course, it is not.

The challenge that you face whenever you move into persuasion is the idea of comfort of your target. People would always want to believe what is comfortably making sense to them, such as their religion, their choice of products, and the entire lifestyle that they subscribe to. Nothing else matters for them. Now, you need to challenge that notion and provide damning evidence that they can be wrong about some (or all) of their beliefs. How do you do that? You need to find a way to make them listen and see to it that you are on the same page, and make them accept that you are making sense. When that happens, you can move in for the kill.

Make the Damaging Admission

One of the most effective ways in persuading your target is by admitting a weakness, downside, drawback or disadvantage in your case or proposal before the other person does. This principle has been known, understood and used for hundreds of years. The reason for admitting a weakness in your case or your claim is that by doing so, you appear to be more credible to the other party or your target.

This will be useful in today's society where everybody is skeptical. By being skeptical, it is meant that people in society today will not usually believe a case or claim if the only benefits, advantages and other arguments in its favor are admitted. As such, expect that people will usually be on the lookout for a catch. In other words, by admitting a negative, flaw or drawback of your claim, proposal or case at the outset, you will be immediately viewed as a person that is honest and trustworthy.

This tactic is one of the best tactics used by most people who pitch their ideas or products. It works well because the seller would always offer a personal testimonial about the product, by making his current experience so much better than his life before. The contrast makes the target very aware of what he wants – he wants to never experience the trouble you went through, and whatever you tested and personally used would save him the trouble.

Why would this tactic work? It makes them aware that you are capable of making mistakes, which make them feel that you do not have your defenses up all the time and that you are able to relax in front of them. In addition, your target will feel more at ease with your presence because you do not appear to be too enthusiastic in persuading him or her to buy your claim, proposal, or case. You are instead, providing them an opening that they can probe. Now, that makes your entire claim a very exciting proposition – it becomes something very interesting that they would want to discover more about. As such, the moment you become trustworthy in your target's eyes is the moment of perfect opportunity to strike!

As an illustrative example, if you have been watching the USA TV legal drama called Law and Order, you will notice that the lawyers in the series usually bring up a small fact that they clearly do not want the other lawyer to bring up during the trial of the case. However, the truth is they really want the lawyer from the opposing side to bring it up so they can also bring up a solid argument that is favorable to them. In other words, bringing up the flaw is really a bait to further their claim! Once the lawyer in the opposing side brings it up during the trial, the flaw or fact will not be as damaging because they had already prepared a counter attack on such claim.

Share a Part of You with Your Target

You can better persuade your target if you performed something that will be favorable to him or her. For example, you can show your confidence to your target by helping him or her with a problem. In other words, put yourself in a situation where you can help him or her in any way that you can. For example, if your target is engaged in selling real estate, stocks or insurance, you can make a phone call to a personal friend regarding the products that your target is trying to sell. If, on the other hand your target is a businessman, offer to distribute his or her business cards to your friends and acquaintances. If your target needs to be introduced to a politician or a policymaker because he or she needs such politician or policymaker to support an environmental or health care cause, by all means introduce the two people to each other. Hence, more than anything else, this means that you will share a part of your time and effort with your target.

Offer your help. Any form of help will be appreciated. In this way, he or she will feel more comfortable with you. Also, your target will feel a certain connection towards you – which means he sees you as just like him or her. Once your target becomes comfortable with you, he or she will lower his or her mental defenses. At the end of the day, once he or she lowers his or her mental defenses, this is the perfect time to persuade him or her in your proposal, claim or case.

Here is what a lot of self-help gurus would do – they give a little background about themselves, and that would always be about the time when they were not successful. They show up and tell you that before they discovered an efficient way to change their lives. They would tell you that their methods worked because they tried doing things the hard way. However, they are willing to show you how to do things that would tremendously improve your life just the way you would like it – the easy way. That tactic appeals to a lot of people because these successful people are willing to share what they have gone through, and that they are willing to share that secret, without the receiver having to go through the bad experiences to gain the knowledge.

It would also be advisable to make it a point that you are also like your target, and that you are offering your claim because you think you are very similar. You can always persuade individuals by making them think that people with the same status or share of experiences would do what you would do. Now, they would find that they can relate to an expert like you!

Knock Their Socks Off

Knocking your target's socks off means that you give him or her a pleasant surprise. How can you do this? Blow your target away with some astonishing fact, an amazing claim or just something that only a few people will be able to know. Make a claim, case or proposal that you will be able to do. Or, you can also show him or her something that has never been done to him or her before. Also, this can be something that can change the way they view your proposal or claim. This will have the effect of opening their minds up in such a way that will make them accept new ideas and thoughts. In other words, this puts them in a state of comfort and reception.

The psychology behind this is that people generally like to be pleasantly surprised. If your target was pleasantly surprised, it will be relatively easy to make him or her say yes to your proposal, claim or case. Do you know why? This is because making a decision to follow another person (you) will always be relatively easier when you help such person discover some amazing new fact. Moreover, making a decision to give in to your claim or proposal will be relatively easy because your target is feeling more comfortable and receptive.

There is a reason why people do believe in success stories – everyone wants to always find the easiest way of doing things, and they are willing to buy whatever a person used to get out of a terrible situation, which is likely to happen to them as well. If you are selling a paracord, that bracelet that people usually use that is made out of strings made to hold a parachute together, keep in mind that they would probably not find themselves jumping out of a plane and using a parachute to save their lives. However, if you tell people that a paracord can hold more than 500 kilos of weight so they can it use to tow their cars, and that it is the preferred bracelet of hunters and adventurers because it can serve as a tourniquet, a fishing line, or something to tie up their tents, they would buy one from you for thrice the price. That is because those are the details that would make them think that your product is much more valuable than it seems.

Another valuable tip related to this persuasion tactic is presenting the proposal that you want to be approved or the product that you want to be bought, last. This means that you have spent a considerable time asking for a proposal to be approved or product to be bought from your target. Because of your efforts, your target normally will be compelled to approve a single item or a single product after dismissing you since the outset of the conversation. As such, it would be strategically beneficial to place your most important proposal or product at the end of the presentation or conversation.

Be Precise

If you want to add an element of believability and credibility to your statements, you should be precise and specific in stating details to your target audience. The reason for this is that if you have precise and specific details in your statements, this means that you know how they affect certain things. If you know how your proposal, claim or case can affect certain things, your statements are harder to attack. In addition, most people unconsciously feel better when they are told of very specific and precise information.

Why do people become convinced by statistics and all sorts of numbers? It is because specific numbers offer them a sense of security. Of course, people do not believe that something would work 100% of the time. They would want something that is almost foolproof, because the "almost perfect" object that they can possibly get is still better than all the other products that they have tried.

For that reason, people also prefer to buy products that use numerical adjectives like most, almost every, or 9 out of 10. But notice the number of questions that you get if you insist that your product is perfect. That is because people do not believe in perfection. They would rather get something that can be flawed, but is still guaranteed to work if they fulfill the given conditions. For people, that makes your product exciting and more credible.

For example, suppose you are an operations management consultant. How can you apply the principle in your dealings with your target? Well, you can tell your target that by availing your consultancy services, his or her sales will increase by 46% in 6 months. Now, that is specific! However, if you tell someone that you can guarantee an increase of a hundred percent in his sales, then your target is more likely to walk away. That is because unless you can show him some big-time client who can back up your story, you are not getting your target as a buyer.

Offer a Benefit

What makes a good offer? An offer should definitely look like it is for the benefit of your target, and not just for your benefit. For that reason, you need to make an offer that would create that same appeal.

Keep in mind that most people are more interested in themselves, and not you. They are more likely to be conscious about themselves, and they would definitely not be after your interests. If you are going to make them act according to what you have in mind, you better make sure that you are making it look like they are getting more benefit than you would.

Why do people buy products from salesmen and become convinced that it is the right decision to do so? The reason is simple – the salesman does not talk about how much commission he would be getting from the sale, and how that profit is going to improve his life. A salesman does not have to beg by mentioning those. However, he would still get to enjoy the benefit of it if he tries to do it from his customer's perspective. All he needs to do is to make it a point that his product is of superior quality, and that the customer would more or less need that item in his life.

The customer, of course, knows that there is something beneficial for the salesman. However, a customer buys without hesitation, because he understands that it is just the way that their roles go. However, if the scene goes with the salesman putting priority on his needs, the customer would definitely want to walk away. When that happens, neither of them would enjoy the benefit.

Now, when it comes to persuading someone that it would be to his benefit to do you a favor, make him a good offer that he would see his benefit first before the reward that you would eventually get.

Seal the Deal

How important is your closing spiel when it comes to persuading someone? In the art of doing magic, it would be the prestige, where the highlight happens. Without a good closer, your effort is not yet certain to come into fruition.

For this reason, it would always be wise to reiterate parts of your conversation wherein you went into some form of agreement. If your target once said in a conversation that he would like to try whatever it is that you are selling, then keep that moment in mind. Before the conversation dies down, make sure that you pull up the closing information. You can say something like this "Since you mentioned that you would like to try Product A, I will go ahead and wrap it for you."

Now, you appeal as a very enthusiastic salesperson with a proactive attitude – something that a lot of customers like. Now, if they refused to have their order wrapped, ask them if you should pack it for them to pick up later. Never say that they have the option to back out of the earlier agreement that you had. Make the target remember that he liked it, and never insinuate that there is an option to say no.

You would be surprised that no matter how old this sales tactic is, it works for almost anything. It is because people are mostly concerned about how to make decision-making a lot easier. Proactive people know that individuals are willing to be bent to your will if they feel that there is someone who is trying to save them from all the bother.

Chapter 19. The 4 Golden Tactics for Deception

In this chapter you will learn:

Get it done easier, faster and better
Induce the sense of scarcity
Relate a friend
Introduce a role model

Get it done easier, faster and better

In this day and age, everybody wants everything to be easier, faster and better. People want things easy because they are basically lazy. People want things fast because they want things now. People want things better because they feel that they deserve to have better things and services.

Look at society today: everything is easy, faster and better. For example, there are the McDonald's and Burger King franchises to provide you with fast food, there is FedEx to provide you with fast packaging and mailing services, there is the Powerball lottery to provide you with a chance to become rich fast, and there are laundry services especially in urban areas to provide you with clean clothes in an hour.

As such, you have to take advantage of this inclination of people. How? Well, the best way to make use of this inclination of people is by promising your target that your business, cause or product will be easier, faster and better than anything else. This is especially true when you are a new player in an industry. The extra effort will make your target desire your proposal more than any proposals that he or she have encountered in the past.

Another way to convince people is to tell them that everyone else around them is most probably using whatever it is you're offering because it provides that rewarding experience of efficiency and practicality. Upon learning that your product is being enjoyed by a lot of other people, it will become clear to your target that it's a smart idea to avail of it as well.

However, you should deliver your promises so the next time your target will need you, he or she will have trust and faith in your capabilities. In addition, you can also take advantage of this inclination by tapping his or her social circle. With this tactic in mind, you would be able to create fads that more people would buy into. That would widen your network and be able to deliver to more people. For example, once you promised to be better and delivered, you can now ask your target to refer you to his or her social circle. This is called the referral system.

The referral system is the easiest way to spread an idea to others by tapping into your target's own network. This is also the way in which you can meet other people and tap into their networks as well. By establishing that you have a superior product or idea and by tapping into multiple persons' social circles, you exponentially spread your interests. Now, that opens up a brand new opportunity for you to influence other people, and that is by introducing the idea that what you are offering is bound to run out soon.

Induce a sense of scarcity

When people know that something they want is limited in terms of time, color, options, availability and quantity, their desire for that something increases exponentially. Correlating to this principle, whenever you desire something but you cannot have it easily, your desire for that object significantly increases. This is nothing but human nature and one of the basic laws of economics.

People have always been aware of the law of supply and demand, and they know how much pain it is to buy something with a much higher price just because the demand for it went up. For that reason, they go to markets in order for them to purchase a product that is more likely to become extremely popular in the future and take advantage of its original price.

Now, many stores are using this tactic – they first get people to understand the inherent value of their product, which they know that the customers would like tremendously. Then, they are going to throw in some freebies and a cheap price, which would make them generate enough profit that would cover their capital. Afterwards, they are going to hide that product from the market, and once they feel that there is enough clamor for the product to come back to the shelves, they are going to put it back on the market at a ridiculously high price.

What does this action do? It makes the storeowner look good by listening to the voice of the people, and then he earns a lot of extra money for doing so. However, he does not need the people to know the second benefit that he enjoyed. All that he would need them to be reminded of is the first benefit. From the point of view of his targets, he is merely trying to make his customers avoid the pain by reintroducing an old product, which would most probably be much pricier compared to the new products that his store is offering. However, the customers did not know that the storeowner has already guaranteed his personal reward – he definitely knows that his old product would sell, no matter what. In fact, he took no risk at all.

Now, how can you take advantage of this principle? The first element of this principle is that your target must be aware that your service, offer, proposal or product is something that will be valuable to him or her. Should he or she lose the opportunity to have this right now, he or she will suffer. The second element is the act of inducement of scarcity. Now, you can induce scarcity to your target. Tell him or her that what you are offering right now will only be available for a limited time, (or in limited quantities, in terms of business operations). By inducing scarcity, your target will realize that there is a real possibility that he or she might not get what she truly desires because time (or stock) will run out fast. As such, it would be crucial to tell your target in no uncertain terms how he or she will lose out in this situation.

As an illustrative example, suppose you are a businessman and your target is a potential customer. You can tell your target that, "I would definitely hate to see you miss out an opportunity to have this latest iPhone! Remember that only 2000 iPhone units of this model will be available. If you wish, I can give you an opportunity to reserve one for yourself!"

That example would work because it involves a specific number, which makes the claim of scarcity appear to be legitimate. A salesman would sell based on how much his target would love or need the product that he offers, and would assert that he is offering it for a certain amount. The thing is that the product is going to be taken off the shelves soon, because it is that special. He can make the claim stronger by saying that most people can only get it on a reservation basis because the competition is very tough, but still, it is so worth it to fight for the product. To increase the pressure on the customer, a storeowner can announce that there is a specific deadline for the customers to make up their minds; missing that deadline is the same as missing the entire opportunity to benefit from the product.

Now, if you were that salesman, you could even improve your pitch by saying that you are willing to go out of your way and make sure that your target would get a fair fighting chance to get that product; however, he should make that effort count. Insinuate that it can be painful for you to go through the hassle of having to fill up the paperwork or to stand in line. Now, you are guaranteed to make a sale, and you'd get a good tip as well.

Limit the Options

There is a known fallacy in logic that people always fall for, and salesmen and magicians love it – it is the fallacy of the limited choice. How you apply it in your trade is really simple – you only offer your target two choices that would always work to your benefit. This works well with the scarcity trick.

You would definitely observe this trick when you are trying to window shop for prices and a salesman approaches you to assist you. After you have found out what benefits you can get, the salesman would always ask you if you want to get that item now, or reserve it for later. Take note that no salesman would ever mention that you could just refuse to take the offer.

The trick is even deeper than it seems. If you said that you are not interested, the salesman would have the right to ask you why you are not buying the product. You, the customer, are bound to feel the pressure because you already agreed to the benefits that are mentioned earlier. You went in on that store aware of the price, and since you like what it does, there is no reason why you should not purchase it.

When the options are limited, most people are bound to act according to the options that they are presented with. Why is that the case? The answer is simple – it's because people are usually too tired to think for themselves.

Relate a friend

It is human nature to like people who are just like you. This is because people have built some trust and comfort with a friend over the years. In addition, people will also follow the behaviors, actions and thought processes of their friends. It is often said that, 'birds of a feather flock together.'

How do you take advantage of this? Suppose you need something from your target – these may refer to the following:

You need to make the target sign and approve your proposal.
You need to make the target purchase your product or avail of your services.

You can simply tell your target that you:

Have already secured the approval of the target's friend beforehand.

Have already sold to the target's friend in the past.

At this point, all you need to do is to make sure that you have the right network to implement this type of strategy. If you are trying to sell a product or an idea to your target, make sure that you can make him aware that you are somehow connected to him via his friend. Suppose you have met your target at a party, ask him about the people he knows. Then scan your mind. If there is a possible person within his friends or acquaintance list that already exists in your contact list, you can use this to support you. You can also go the other way around – you can ask him if he knows a friend that is also in his circle.

Now, the manipulation starts when you explain how your friend, a.k.a. Person A, is very similar to your target. Note all their similarities – how they choose food, how they see to it that they get a promotion, etc. As much as possible, paint a very vivid picture in his head about their similarities, and how they are very likely to have the same solution for most problems.

After doing so, introduce a problem, particularly a problem that your target does not know how to solve yet. Or better yet, introduce a problem that would involve your product or that your idea would most definitely solve.

Now, the goal is to make your target feel that someone he knows, who acts very similarly to him, bought your product, and has been enjoying the benefits since he did. Since you have painted a picture of their similarity, the target would hate to feel that someone who just earns the same amount of money or goes to the same workplace has been able to practically solve a problem, and that he did not. You can insinuate the idea that he does not have to miss out on the opportunity that you are offering – if his friend could, then he can. Make him feel that you are on his side – not are you only willing to help him solve your problem, you can also share some other things that involve your product that his friend probably didn't know.

As you can see, most people would want to come up with the same solution to simple and complex life problems the same way their peers would. However, they would also want to discover the better way of doing things. That means that if you showed your target that there is actually a more efficient way of using your product, he would be more inclined to buy that from you, just because he wants to get the friendly upper hand.

Introduce a Role Model

Role models are most often the quintessential part of advertising; that is why people who are in commercials are often good looking, or they appear to be always making the smarter choice. People, like those who are in the commercials, will always want to enjoy the better and more positive side of life. For that reason, if you were trying to plant an idea or if you are trying to sell something, take advantage of the fact that most people would want to play an important role. The only way they can do that is to take after a role model.

Imagine that you are in a bar and you are sitting next to a handsome young man who looks like he has power over women. True enough, he can send drinks to whatever table he points to and gets the results that he wants –he gets ladies' numbers, and some are actually approaching him. You would also want to get the time and attention of a random beautiful woman. If you feel that this role model, sitting at the bar, is getting all that self-esteem from his drink, what are you most likely to do? You are most likely to say this: "I'd get what he's having."

Now, how do you apply this scene to your art of manipulation? You can introduce a role model to your target. However, a role model is not like anyone else. He must offer a benefit that only he can offer at the moment. At the same time, he has to be a person who does things like an expert would.

How does a role model enter into the story of a deception? Role models are always the authority that every deceptive person takes advantage of. The reason is simple – everybody would want to believe the expert, and everybody wants to buy whatever there is in a powerful person's arsenal.

Now, if you have the qualities of a leader or you can act like one, you definitely would have leverage in any argument. By establishing that you are a subject matter expert, you are definitely going to make the most believable claim. That is because everything that you say becomes an almost instant valid claim. Since you have established that you have always been knowledgeable about the topic at hand, you will always have the upper hand.

It is because even if you do not win the argument with your target, you would definitely still be able to influence other people in the vicinity. By maximizing the number of targets subjected to your deception, you will be able to manipulate all the other people that surround your main target; in effect, you increase the likelihood of making them do the job of convincing your main target.

Have you ever heard of cognitive dissonance? That is the trick that your mind experiences when you believe in something, but other people around you are all saying otherwise. For example, if a teacher in a class you are in asks the question, to which you believe the right answer is A, and the entire class says that it should be B, you feel confused and uncomfortable. It is because, even though you are certain that you are making the right decision, your body begins to react differently. What happens is you give out a different answer just to feel like all the others. In the end, you are almost bound to give B as an answer just to escape the pressure of being different.

Managing Deception

When you use the tactics that are mentioned above, you will be creating an environment for your target that makes him perceive the world around him in a light that is very far from the truth. Looking at these tactics closely, you will see that you manage to achieve deception when you are able to convince your target to look at ANOTHER POSSIBILITY, based on how he looks at the entirely new environment that you have enclosed him in. You can manage to achieve that with the right combination of persuasion and manipulation.

Deceptions are not really designed to have a lasting impact on your target, but how it would appeal to him would be based largely on how you manage to make him stick to the environment that you introduced him to. If you want your deception to last, you would need to convince your target into the realization that believing the lie is very comfortable for him. Even though he would come to the realization that he has fallen into a trap, he would also realize that it is too much bother to actually figure out the truth. Look at how magic tricks work – they are easily figured out as mere mind tricks, but not everyone would want to actually dig into where the trick is really happening. Fans of magic would largely want to watch it happen, rather than make it happen. They are already satisfied with the feelings of amazement that they experience whenever they witness well-executed tricks.

At this point, you already know the basics of manipulation, persuasion and deception and can do first level tricks. Now, it's time for you to learn how you can make use of these concepts and turn them into powerful combinations that will enable you to gain massive profit.

Chapter 20. The Secret of Pacing and Leading

When you are trying to build rapport and get your audience to follow your lead, there are two main techniques that you have to employ. They are pacing and leading, which enables people to build confidence and trust around you and allow themselves to go in the direction you want them to go. These techniques would be very helpful in most situations where you need people to agree with you and begin seeing things your way.

Why is it Beneficial?

Most people think that they do not want their emotions and thoughts manipulated, but somehow, they would actually need a person that can influence them into thinking which direction they are most likely be willing to go. They have to accept, however, that it is not always the case that they can make a conscious decision knowing what is going to do them good. You, however, can make them go to a direction that they want at a faster speed.

Pacing and leading works like a dance – it takes two people in agreement in order for it to work, which involves another important element: compromise. Without harmony between two people, they will not go anywhere that isn't mutually beneficial for them. Like in any relationship, they would be stuck in a rut.

With this, you will know that being able to "manipulate" people into your line of thinking is more like entering into an agreement with them, and allowing their subconscious to make perfect sense of their actions by helping them build a new comfort zone, which is when they are around you. You will also figure out that once they are comfortable, they are much easier to manipulate.

More about Mirroring

Mirroring, a technique used to build rapport discussed in an earlier chapter, is a key practice that you need to master in order for you to introduce rapport in every interaction you have with other people. Mirroring is also termed pacing by some practitioners of Neuro Linguistic Programming, which defines it as the practice of matching the actions and behavior of your audience in order to introduce trust into your interaction. With that said, that means that being able to match your audience allows you to break down their barriers, which allows you to introduce rapport.

Why do you need to match another person's behavior or actions? Let's use the example of attending a black tie event. Most people would prefer to still wear formal clothes to attend such event, even if the invitation did not specify that it is a requirement for them to do so. They would find the extra time and effort to make sure that they are going to appear at the event in their best tuxedo or gown, because they feel that they are going to look different from the crowd if they did not do so. At the same time, you will find yourself being looked over from head to toe if you should ever go to that event in casual clothes. You will also find out soon that no one wants to talk to you if you are dressed differently.

When you think about that situation, you'd find that most people would actually want to engage a person that is similar to them. Billionaires often hang out with billionaires, and actors with fellow actors. It is not to promote segregation and shun diversity, but that is just plain human nature. People tend to hang out with people who they think can understand their beliefs and lifestyle.

If you have the nasty habit of smoking, you might find a silver lining in indulging in that vice – people who smoke with their clients or bosses are mostly those who are bound to get the upper hand in closing deals or getting promotions in the long run. It does not mean that they are more competent, but rather, they are the ones who are able to establish rapport with their target. Who knew that you could get that much out of a single vice?

Essentially, mirroring or pacing is following the behavior of your target that is essential to your mission. You need to understand which part of their behavior would matter the most to them – if you want to build a rapport with a musician, you would most possibly to listen to the kind of music that they like. You would want to take cues from your specific target on what could possibly make them pay attention to you. Now, when they know that you know that you possibly speak their language, you would be able to lead them in any direction that you want them to go.

So what makes similarity that your target perceives that you have lead to the element of trust? The answer is simple – people want to trust something that offers them comfort. That familiarity that you are willing to offer them offers them that, because it makes them avoid the convoluted relationship of people that have different ways of approaching life. People normally root for people that can offer them any reason to think that they are one of them.

However, there is such a thing as too much pacing, which makes your effort to establish rapport too obvious. For example, you would find that trying to talk to people about every common interest that you have, or trying to buy the same clothes that they wear would soon make them irritated with your presence. They may begin by being straightforward to get whatever business you have done – but they may question what you want out of them, and begin to raise their defenses around you. With that in mind, remember that the best kind of pacing is being able to get the results that you want to get from your target without being noticed as being too obvious in your attempt to "belong".

How You Can Perfect Pacing

There are many ways to make sure that your target does not notice that you are subconsciously establishing rapport. Here are some of the aspects that you can pace with, which allows you to mirror your target without being too obvious that you are trying to win him over.

1. Body posture

Posture is a good determiner of a person's mood, and being able to mirror the way a person sits or stands sets you into the mode of being the empathizer. If you are trying to talk to a guy sitting in a bar to offer him anything, you can sit a few seats apart from him and order what he is drinking from the bartender. If your target is slouching, slouch too, but appear like you are not paying attention to him. It would make him notice you from the corner of his eye, and start an empathic conversation. He might ask you how your day is going. That is your cue to start a conversation.

2. Figures of speech, metaphors, or specific phrases

If you listen to a group of people for a few minutes, you will find out that every person in that room has a specific choice of words for describing or naming things. Some may like to use the word "that stuff" to refer to a group of objects that he can't remember the proper term for, or they may use the word "bunch". Now, when you want to establish rapport to specific people in that group, make sure that you also use the words that they repeatedly say. That would prompt them to invite you to join their conversation!

3. Personal style

Don't you ever wonder why people tend to always say, "I'll have what he's having" in a bar to establish a conversation? At the same time, do you notice that it would be their target that is most likely to say the first word to them? This applies not only in the bar setting. This technique is also very applicable in malls and other locations that would have two or more people trying to establish rapport with each other.

4. Tone, accent, and tempo

It is no secret that people with specific speech patterns because of their linguistic upbringing are those people who typically end up talking to each other. If you are good with manipulating your speech patterns, accent, and talking speed, then you can use this mirroring technique to establish a rapport with people in different locations or ethno linguistic origins.

At the same time, it also pays to pay attention to the voice tone and tempo of the person that you are talking to. You may notice that some people would have difficulty trying to understand what you are saying when you do not match with the way they speak. The key is this – if you feel that your target can understand you better when you match their speaking tone or tempo, do it.

5. Orientation towards career, time, or life

You may observe that different people with different jobs have specific word choices when it comes to work, schedules, or even how they describe their objectives. For example, people who work in an office are most likely to always address future tasks to belong to tomorrow, but most freelancers are likely to think of work to be happening on a specific schedule. You may also notice that business owners tend to think about the profit that they make, while employees tend to think about the amount of salary that they get according to payout cutoffs. With that in mind, you can sell a product to these people in terms of how they normally view money or the type of their orientation for time.

6. Personal values

One of the time-tested approaches to establishing a rapport is to pace with one's biases, political and religious views, and orientation towards pop culture. In the US, for example, people tend to group themselves as Democrats or Republicans. You may find that these people have separate views on the separation of church and state, as well as opinions regarding gender roles. If you want to establish rapport with anyone who belongs to either group, you have to pace with their approach regarding worldviews, or you would not be able to enter into any compromise with them.

Mirroring Magic Tricks

When you mirror your target for a considerable amount of time, say 30 minutes, you may find that you are able to pace with him unconsciously, even when you get separated within a room. You would notice that you are able to "inherit" some of his traits, such as his most subtle movements or his manner of speaking, even if those are not the actions or behaviors that you are not trying to pace with. Some books of NLP techniques would tell you that this is perfectly normal – by only locking in on certain action patterns of your target, there is a big tendency that you would be able to subconsciously mirror his behavior, which makes it very natural for you to build a rapport afterwards.

At the same time, research tells us that pacing with a target would also allow one to "know" certain things about the subject, and it would be much easier to get confirmation about this knowledge afterwards. You may also feel that after pacing with a person for some time, you are able to establish a rapport with your target, even from across the room!

Leading

Now here is the part where you try to reap the rewards of pacing, which is leading. Essentially, leading refers to the act where you can deliberately move another person's actions or beliefs to a goal that you have in mind.

When you have been pacing with a person for some time, you will feel that when you change your movement, your target begins to follow you, as if he is "following your lead." You may try this simple exercise to see if your pacing techniques and attempt to lead is working:

Walk with your target and mirror his posture and walking pace. Follow the way he sways his arms and make sure that you are able to mirror most of his subtle movements. When you feel that you are already in sync, deliberately change the way you move, e.g. switch the footing of the steps or walk faster. You will notice that your target will subconsciously imitate your movements, and he will believe that he is the one setting that movement.

The good thing is that leading does not only affect your target's movement. If you are pacing with his language and the rest of his actions, you may find that you can actually create the decision and action that you want to get from him! That means that after building a rapport and syncing with your target, you can effectively persuade him into your line of thinking.

You may find that a careful balance of rapport and leading can get you the results that you desire. You may also see that there are certain linguistic approaches in order for you to command that person to initiate a change in their behavior. The use of verbs, for example, creates that mental energy needed to initiate change. With the use of action words, the mental energy created can help your target to create the action that you desire, because your target would want to create the physical action to match with their thoughts.

However, just like in pacing, leading requires great subtlety in order for you to avoid any possible resistance from your target. If that happens, make sure that you pace with them again before using triggers in order for them to make the proper order of reasoning for the change of your behavior. You will be able to notice that as long as you go back to syncing with their independent actions, you will have the ultimate leverage in persuading people to think the way you do! Be careful in your imitation not to make him feel that you are making fun of him or you lose the impetus.

Chapter 21: The Art of Selling

Selling is the interesting mixture of persuasion, manipulation and deception. When you are able to master these techniques, you will be able to harness unlimited leverage when it comes to selling any product to any type of client that you may possibly encounter.

What You Need to Sell First

When it comes to sales, you have to keep in mind that the most important commodity that you have to offer your client is yourself. People are only willing to comply and agree that you are able to bend their mind into agreeing with you if you are able to see to it that you can make them accept you as a seller. In essence, you are trying to make them agree first to the fact that a person like you is going to do something for them. If they don't, you would have to go back to an earlier stage of establishing rapport. The rapport includes convincing them that you are right person to sell them what they want.

If you have not sold anything in the past, that hardly matters. People are not looking at your track record or how many times you have been promoted – they are just looking at you. They would only want to be able to trust that you are a person worthy of their time.

Selling yourself rather than paying a lot of attention to what you are supposed to offer a potential customer goes a longer way – there are many occasions where customers may not find that they need the stuff that they order, but they try to make logical sense of the purchase by establishing that the item will be useful to them one day, just because the salesman told them that would be the case. At the same time, they are more likely to buy from you again, no matter what you are selling in the future. In that sense, being able to sell yourself allows you to enjoy an advantage over people who offer similar products or ideas over a prolonged period of time.

Understanding What Makes People Buy

Why do people want to get something from a store? Their process of thought is really simple – they try to make logical explanation for their decisions, no matter what that item is. They would create a world inside their heads in which all their decisions make perfect sense, and no matter what happens, they will try to defend their decision. That matters in a similar way to their decisions about their relationships with other people.

The problem that you are most likely to encounter whenever you offer yourself and your ideas to someone is this: people convince themselves that they are right after they have made the decision. That means that after they have accepted an offer, they will most likely stick to that decision. But getting to that part is the hardest part. The good news is that there is a workaround for this problem. If you are having a hard time trying to convince them that they would never regret having made that decision, you place their mindset in the future, where they can feel safe that they will definitely not regret accepting the offer that you have for them.

How do you do that? It is simple: every person has a specific buying pattern, which they use again and again because they know what gives them the best and the least disappointing results. In order to take advantage of that, know the things that they are most likely to buy and relate your offer to that. The clue to their buying formula is hidden in the choice of words; so pay attention to that.

For example, if you are trying to sell a car to someone, you might want to find out their experience when they last bought one. Ask them the reason why they bought that car in the first place. If they said that they loved their old car because of its looks, then you know how to make the right approach – all you need to tell them is that the car that you are offering has a sleek design that they are going to love. That solves the first part of figuring out their buying formula, which tells you that they are most likely to buy items that appeal to their visual senses. Now, if they tell you that their old car was beautiful and then they fell instantly fell in love with it, you know what their visual reaction to anything does and how they see it when looking back into the past. Now you know that every time you sell them something that appeals to their visual aesthetic senses, they are not likely to regret it!

However, you may not get a direct answer from a person that you are targeting. The reason for that is that a lot of people do not even realize that there is a reason for their behavior, or they cannot remember the feeling anymore. Now, what you need to pay attention to is their body language along with their linguistic preferences. If they said that they bought their old car because they liked the way it looked when they first saw it, yet you see that their eyes are looking downward, or that they are fiddling with something with their hands, you would figure out that he/she is the kind of person who is more likely to buy things that they can manipulate or touch, and that they are more in touch with their emotions. The best way to appeal to them is to describe the emotions that they are most likely to feel when they say yes to what you are offering them.

Chapter 22. How to Ensure Your Offer Appeals

When you are trying to persuade someone to listen to your ideas and accept them with an open mind, you need to make sure that you are able to follow certain steps in order for you to be able to "close" the deal. The following steps would allow you to have the opportunity to present yourself and your idea, build a relationship, and then lead them to the action that you want to achieve.

1. Get the Invitation

It may be perceived that salesmen and vampires are alike – they need an invitation to be able to enter someone's territory. However, that is the same for most people. No one would be able to build any type relationship without having the other person open himself up to any possible change.

However, you will notice that it is not always easy to get invited into other people's lives – when you want to open a conversation with someone, you will often have to endure their heightened resistance, and you can probably guess what happens next – the other person is just waiting for you to launch into your well-rehearsed opening in order for him to say "No, I'm not interested."

So what do you do to get your opening past the initial "Hello" stage and start persuading that other person that you are worthy of his time? What you need to do is to start mirroring him in order for you to build an initial relationship. However, you might find it challenging to do that when you are trying to sell anything – over the phone, you have to get the invitation within 15 seconds before your selling tactic becomes threatened. Face-to-face, you have a little more time to get the invite, since you can effectively mirror them within 2-3 minutes and secure the right to continue with your proposition.

2. Build your rapport

Once your target has come to the conclusion that you are worthy of his time, it is time to nourish that initial relationship by carefully pacing with him. The idea of building rapport with pacing is to ensure that you will be able to build that relationship quickly and establish that you are a person that your target can trust. However, make sure that you don't move towards your main goal too quickly or too slowly, otherwise, you will lose the relationship. When you lose that relationship, you are not only losing the invitation from that person, but also create resistance as well.

You will know that you have successfully built a relationship when the target is beginning to confide in you about his needs, and it follows that whenever you propose anything, you will find that there is little or no resistance at all.

3. Offer your idea through consultation

People are not gullible and empty-headed – no matter whom they are or how clueless they appear, they would still want to make sure that they had a hand in their decisions. They do not want other people to make their decisions for them. That is why asking them to agree with you in a form of consultation basis is the best move that you can make. However, you can only go through this phase when you and your target have already entered a relationship and a clear commitment to compromise has been established.

Since consultation is really an exchange of information, this is also the point where you would encounter objections from your target. However, you need to see that those objections present you an opportunity to clarify the benefits that you are trying to present. You will also find that you will be able to explain yourself better and handle objections more efficiently when you have secured a relationship that is built on mutual trust.

However, you may find that continuous consultation may create a resistance where you know that you cannot continue offering your idea anymore to your target. When he says, “Let me think about it” you know that he doesn’t want to listen any more. However, you can secure an invitation instead to make your relationship stronger. That would rekindle his commitment to you and make him more likely to compromise.

4. Reinforce your bond

When you live in an ideal world, you can easily get what you want out of a deal from people, once you get them to open up to you. However, it rarely happens. At one time or another, you will have to reveal parts of your offer that may not suit your target, and sometimes that ends up with your target backing off from whatever you have to say. To prevent that from happening, see to it that you continuously create rapport with your target in order for them to see that you will come up with a positive solution to their problems within the terms of your offer. That means you are listening to them and hear what they say. That reinforces bonds.

Remember that being consultative and trying to reinforce a positive relationship means different things. Reinforcing your relationship while you are trying to make an offer means putting your target’s share of benefits before yours, which makes your target feel that you are willing to think of his comfort before taking care of your own needs. While you are doing this, you also think of your leverage – the more comfortable your target feels around you, the least resistance you are going to get when you push your offer back to the table.

5. Push for a decision

Closing in on your target is the easiest step in this process when you have been successful in building a positive relationship with your target. If you have been able to lead your target through a very effective exchange of information and ideas, you probably have a logical outcome in mind.

However, if you know that you have been experiencing different scenarios that prevent you from closing the deal successfully, you should aim to close it while still building your relationship. You need to push for a decision that will lead to another appointment, and another invitation for you to offer your ideas. At the same time, you may also opt to go for a close that will lead to an agreement that would still be very beneficial to you, such as securing an appointment with your target's boss, or to present your ideas to a deciding committee. That will lead you to getting the opportunity to having the invitation to sell to the bigger fish!

When you think about it, it is only possible for you to push for a decision that would conform to the type of relationship that you have built. There are times that you have to agree to your target's decision to maintain the traditional roles of the savvy buyer or the purchasing agent, because you prompted them to do so and they need to create resistance in order to protect their own interests. When this happens, you have to keep in mind that you need to determine the outcome of the engagement while you are trying to exchange information with the target and while you are building rapport.

Also remember that you have to be flexible with your objectives and make them conform to events that are about to happen. During an engagement with a target, you may have initially started out thinking that it would be easy to get a contract with him. During the appointment, you may find out that the best deal that you can get out of him is to secure an appointment with his boss, who has the upper hand when it comes to getting you the deal that you want.

As you practice more, you will find out that you are able to redefine your objectives more quickly even during the shortest of discussions with future contacts. This will enable you to get the most out of your time and always determine the best way to grow your network.

Chapter 23. The Magic of Language Preference

When you are trying to get another person to agree with you, you may sometimes find that after an exhaustive onslaught of thoughts from you, you feel like you are talking to a total brick wall. Then you may hear another person giving the same spiel that you did, but instead, get a positive response. What made the difference?

The words that you choose can either create trust or resistance. When you manage to create trust from your audience, they suspend their judgment and gain confidence, making them listen to anything that you have to say. However, if you invite resistance, you will not be able to have the opportunity to be listened to by your target.

The Power of the Common Denominator

The best way to establish a positive connection with your chosen audience is to always find the common denominator. By looking for your shared interest or by creating an image that makes you appear similar to them, you are more likely to be a credible person to your target.

If you see commercials that aim to sell a product to different people, you will always see that they are trying to say that no matter how diverse a community is, people will always root for that one product that brings them together. With that said, most people are trying to sell this idea: no matter how different people are, they can be able to offer something that provides for a common goal. When you sell ideas in that way, you will be able to reach out for the human desire to belong and become a part of a meaningful group. That diminishes the risk of getting objections, because you are appealing to a person's sense of belonging. People will always respond to you positively because they will see that you are willing to share their values and interests, and since you are just like them, you are more likely to understand their needs.

Why Most People Fail the Common Denominator Approach

There are a lot of people who want to manipulate or persuade people who are using this approach the wrong way. What they do is this: they obviously spy on people and feign interest, without even meaning it. They see a picture hanging on their target's home that shows a mountain climbing expedition, and they instantly pretend that they have deep passion for that activity, without even knowing what hiking shoes look like. However, most of these people fail to acknowledge that people can see what's fake or not, and their targets instantly smell manipulation and deceit. Instead of building a positive relationship, pretending to have a common denominator without a semblance of truth can build walls and barriers you will never knock down.

If you are trying to find a common denominator with your target and it seems like you can't find anything in common with you, try a different approach. You can still make them feel that you belong in the same group if you choose the right words that would make your target think that you are speaking the way he does or in his language.

The Language Choice

Your choice of words, whether verbal or written, did not occur to you randomly. You definitely have a reason why you talk the way you do. When you think about it, you choose your words because it allows you to respond within the environment that you are in. At the same time, you only choose to respond to words that you are familiar with, or statements that you know refer to the things that you know.

The same goes for other people. When you go to other countries, you know that people are welcoming to you if they are trying to teach you how to speak their language, or when they make the effort to talk to you in English. However, you are very aware that they do not want you inside their homes and establishments when they are trying not to include you in a conversation by using words that are entirely foreign to you. When people use unfamiliar words, you know that there is hostility. Just the way people talk around you triggers uncomfortable feelings.

So here is something that you have to keep in mind: people like to believe in you and trust you with anything that they have as long as they like you. If a person does not know you at all, he will create an impression of you inside his head according to the words that you utter. You may make it a point that you look presentable in order to look convincing, but people do not really trust a handsome man that does not speak their language.

How to Take Advantage of Language as a Tool

People often respond according to the senses that they use. You may categorize people to be visual, auditory or kinesthetic. Here is how you can use language to your advantage when trying to sell these people any idea or product.

1. For Visual People

If you are trying to convince a visual person that you are right, think that they tend to get ideas better when they "see the entire picture." You may notice that people who are visual tend to leave out some phrases and words, as if they are trying to make you imagine. You may think that they sound choppy when they speak, but they have the entire idea in their heads. However, they may fail to verbalize their ideas, because most of the time, they can't find the right words to say what's on their mind.

Here's how to match their language: make use of a lot of visual words, and they will feel that you are confidently saying what's on their mind. If that is not the case, they will feel that you are trying to verbalize something that you also picture, and that creates the rapport that you need.

It would also help if you aid them by using graphs, charts, or any visual representation of the message that you are trying to say. They are more likely to believe you if they see data that you are trying to impart.

2. For Auditory People

Auditory people are the ones that are more likely to be convinced if they hear the information, and they are more likely to like you if you match their tone, and you affirm them by saying phrases like "sounds good to me" or "that statement rings true." You can spot them easily when you hear people trying to explain a statement according to how it sounded to them. They are also the ones who use alliterations and rhymes a lot, because they want a musical ring to their statements. These are the people who like the sound of their own voices. While they can be good listeners, they are in complete contrast with the visual people – they tend to talk a lot. That means that talking to them would be to a great advantage because you can get a lot of clues regarding their preferences and values.

When you are trying to appeal to an auditory target, you may prefer to use the techniques used in most auditory self-help books. Notice that they are mostly packaged with rhyming or alliterative titles, such as The Power of Predictive Persuasion. Should you want to create a powerful impact on your target, make sure that you are gunning for music and words.

Auditory people are also the type of people who want opportunities for a dialogue. They will not want to read manuals and they are not likely to pay attention to any charts, even if the information is right there. They would rather hear it from you, and they will only look at these details on paper if you link the materials that you are trying to present to them in the conversation that you have with them. They would treat that as a verbal clue, as if they are in a game.

You would also want to open up with quotes, or a similar statement that go well with your argument, preferably from someone that they respect. Should you sell them anything, make sure that you pepper your discussion with testimonials. At the same time, keep in mind that should you need to update them, they prefer that you call them instead of sending an email. They would definitely want to hear from you.

3. For Kinesthetic People

Kinesthetic people are those types of possible targets that really like action, or any activity that would make them feel something. They tend to understand you better if you discuss your argument with them by making them imagine and experience the situation within their minds. They are also the types of people who tend to raise questions over and over again until they can trigger an appropriate reaction or a feeling that can help them connect to your ideas.

Keep in mind that kinesthetic people are those who generally appear to have a short attention span. They tend to move – they keep on stretching their legs and arms every minute and they seem like they can't stay seated for a very long time.

They are the ones who always ask for breaks during seminars. You can also spot them easily by finding people who tend to be pushy or intrusive of personal space.

When dealing with this type of target, make sure that you keep your argument very short and sweet. They want the conversation short, but they also want to hear the complete details – they want hear the specifics and they need them fast. If they do not feel that everything is right there in front of them, they will ask others to deal with the details instead. That means that they tend to jump to conclusions based on their initial reaction, and they tend to think that everything is done before they are aware of everything that they need to know. However, keep in mind that you need to be patient with them – they are very quick to perceive and react to tension.

If you want to keep talking to a kinesthetic person, make sure that you give them an activity to keep their body busy and to make them focus their attention on you. Make sure that you deal with them face-to-face in order to ensure that they have not drifted off to tend to other things in their thoughts, or are too busy trying to assess their feelings. They are also the ones who like comfort a lot, so it may be a good idea to take them out for dinner or coffee.

Bonus: How to Pace in a Digital World

Here's something new – digital pacing. You may find it useful to know how to build rapport in this day and age, especially since people tend to find information and people by using digital means. However, keep in mind that pacing through use of websites or emails would enable you to help your target rationalize the decision that you want them to make, but it cannot possibly sustain a positive relationship. It would still be better to correspond or talk to your target so you can observe their behavior and their preferences when you are trying to build mutual trust.

So why learn about this? Sounding like you belong to modernity and that you are business and tech savvy can greatly contribute to your credibility. It makes the target aware that you have substantial information about what you are saying, and you have read or provided good content about it on the Internet. It also makes you appear up to date, and shows that you have the ability to update the information that they have about the topic at hand, which can renew their belief in you.

Should you want to use this to your advantage, make sure that you initially pace with your target through visual, auditory, or kinesthetic means. At the middle of the engagement, insert digital pacing to increase your credibility. Afterwards, resume pacing with them using visual, auditory, or kinesthetic language. Thus, use digital means to back up what you have to say, but never ignore their presence or the type of conversation that they respond well to.

Keep in mind that when you pace with different people, remember to subconsciously make their language sound natural in your head. Allow them to somehow change your natural tone, in order for you to truly speak their language. Doing so will prevent you from sounding tongue-tied or clumsy. That will not only protect your comfort, but will also assure your target that you are eloquent with the personal language he chose. Also, make sure that you make your statements simple. Remember that you do not have to have all the words in order to communicate. All you need is to speak in a way that fits with your target's actions.

Now you know techniques that will break personal barriers so you can make an opening to push people for actions that will be favorable to you, you now enjoy unlimited advantage over most people that you know or will meet. You have the power to make everyone believe that you are always credible, which makes you very capable of deceit, persuasion, or even of manipulating people. It will be the last thing that they will expect, since they already have trust in what you say.

Keep in mind that practicing all the techniques discussed in this book will not only improve the way you switch from one language preference to another, but also to keep you from losing sight of your goal. Always remember that you need to master awareness that you have already succeeded in building the right relationship in order for you to lead the other person into making the decision that you want. Once you have mastered that skill, you will be able to effectively work with people's minds and make them more than willing to help you fulfill your personal goals.

Chapter 24. Deception Through Gas Lighting

It is almost impossible to break someone's walls when he is certain about his own convictions. You may encounter impossible people that would willingly bring you to court or challenge you to an endless debate just to prove that he is right. When things come to this point, there is a technique used by many manipulators when they feel that they are in a bad position when it comes to convincing their targets. This technique is called gas lighting.

The Power of Self-Doubt

Gas lighting as a term is believed to have originated from a stage play wherein a character makes his wife believe that she is going insane by subtly changing her environment, which would involve slowly making the flame on her gas lamp go dim. Now, the term is used to describe techniques devised by manipulators to establish doubt in their target's minds in order for them to step in and gain control of the situation.

The technique is sophisticated and it takes a while before it may work when you do not know the target that well. However, if you are very good at playing poker, you may feel that this is part of any game that requires some mental trickery.

The main element of this mind trick is the mentalist's ability to establish doubt in the mind of his target. However, it is more than the doubt that you feel when you think that you are being lied to. When you perform this technique, you are establishing to your target that he may not be fit to make a decision, hence, the establishment of self-doubt.

When a person doubts himself, the punishment that he creates against himself goes a long way. The mere fact that he cannot trust his own judgment produces great anxiety. When one is not sure about the consequences of his actions, he is led to do one thing, which is to search for another solution. The manipulator easily comes in and tells his target what to do.

How to Do Gas Lighting

There are several factors that you need to consider when you do gas lighting. The key to perform it successfully is to establish the following:

1. A series of truths and vague untruths

When you want to change the environment of the target and make him believe that the conditions have already changed, then you need to create a list of true things. For example, you know that you are inside your room when you see your favorite pillow on your bed, or when you see your personal lampshade. However, you feel that you are not there when you do not see them. If these things are transferred into another room with the same layout, you can easily be misled into thinking that that different room is yours. How would you feel when you are told that you entered the wrong room? You become anxious at the thought of it. The next time you enter your true room, you would feel paranoid. You feel that someone might be playing tricks on you again.

2. The establishment of yourself as an authority

To assume the role of the manipulator, you need to make sure that your target believes you when he is not sure of his own judgment. Following the above example, when you change the layout of your target's bedroom and he is not sure whether he is entering the right room or not, you should assume authority that you know that it is his. Tell him another series of truths, for example that he is in the right room, or that someone just changed the bed sheets. Tell him where his pillow is. Because of his anxiety, he is likely to believe you when you give the proof that you actually know what is going on.

3. The direction you need the target to follow

Think of the situation wherein your target is unsure of whether he is in his own room or not as a proof that he needs to doubt himself and seek your advice whenever he enters his house. Establishing a similar scenario would allow you to have a playing card in your hand whenever you need to drive your target in a specific direction. You can always say that previously he was not sure about where he was, and that is also the situation now. Since you have established yourself as the person who knows the truth, he would be bound to ask for your help. At this point, you can tell him what you want him to believe, and following that, what he should do next.

The Manipulator as the Shedder of Light

Gas lighting as a deception technique will only work if you are able to make it a point that your target will believe that you are the only one who can tell him what to do and that you are the only one who can tell what is true or not. In a lot of situations, being the most credible person in the room is difficult to achieve. For that reason, it is very important that you plant the seeds of your credibility.

It also means that performing this trick can be very difficult or time-consuming, since it may require you to subtly imply to the target that he is wrong and you are always right. Doing so would require you to make changes to his environment little by little, and then point them out whenever you do so. It is like teaching your target how to learn a different language or how to use a code. In a way, it may require you to actually alter what he knows about himself and how he should react to things that he normally encounters.

While this technique may take a long while to be perfected, it provides a strong hold on your target's belief, and like any great deception, the changes that he went through and how you staged all of them would be very hard for him to detect. You are the only one who really knows what's going on, and even bystanders cannot see all the things that you have done in order to perform the trick. Since you are the only one who knows all the elements in his environment that you managed to change little by little, it becomes easy for your target to just surrender to everything that you are saying and uphold them as the truth.

When you think about it, this same technique is used by most mentalists and street magicians who have already set up the stage to any unsuspecting target. While their targets think that they see an ordinary box or ordinary deck of cards that might have a bit of surprise, they do not really look at where the deception is happening. By being able to make targets focus on another thing that is suspicious, the "magic" is already happening somewhere else that is undetectable. The magician makes a number of true statements, and then when the trick is performed, the target will always question what he just saw. Because he cannot tell how the trick was performed and when exactly the deception occurred, he just surrenders to the thought that it is, in fact, magic.

However, when you perform gas lighting over an extended amount of time, you risk the danger of exposing where the trick is happening, but when you get past that risk and the traps go unnoticed, you can perform this technique again and again to the unsuspecting target. It is like stealing credit card information and making little purchases that are hard to notice. When the bill arrives and the credit card owner wonders why he needs to pay more than he usually does, he is bound to look on the statement for large purchases, which of course, he made himself. Should he suspect that something is wrong and he asks the manipulator, he would still be made to look for the larger charges and be convinced that it is his own fault that the bill is more than usual. Why gas lighting always works is because you tell the truth, but not its entirety. The main part of the deceit is to hide the little, often harmless lies, that when put together, create an elaborate deception that is enough to make the target confuse reality with fabrication.

Practical Uses of Gas Lighting

This technique has a lot of practical forms, but it is particularly useful when you are defending yourself from any accusation. For example, if someone accuses you of lying, you can make use of gas lighting to make that statement backfire on your accuser by proving that there have been circumstances wherein he was not sure whether he knew the truth or not, and you are the one who can tell him. By saying so, you make it seem to him that it is unreasonable for him to make his claim when he was not even sure what the truth was.

You will probably encounter this technique in courtrooms, where lawyers throw in this trick in order to discredit a witness. By saying that the witness has bouts of paranoia or has a previous history where he cannot even tell whether he is in good mental health, his credibility is shattered. The lawyer that is interrogating him easily manipulates him into retracting what he just said, or agreeing to another truth. Even if the witness refuses to agree to what the lawyer is trying to establish, there is still leverage for the interrogating side, and that damages the reputation of the witness.

Even if you are not practicing law, you can take advantage of the positive results that this brings you when you are in sales or in customer service. There are a lot of situations where customers complain about products, without having first read the manual or turning the item on. When you state the fact that there are many situations where customers do not use the product for its intended purpose, or that many have failed to follow simple instructions which would solve more than 90% of the problem, they will begin to doubt themselves and the real reason why they are making a complaint in the first place. What they are likely to do is to end the call and think where they could possibly have gone wrong. Not only would that save you time trying to repeat instructions that they could find by themselves, you possibly do them a service by making them find solutions instead of you.

Some Notes to Keep in Mind

You need to take a lot of caution when you use gas lighting – it can backfire on you if you try to do the trick too quickly. The reason is that anyone can discover major environmental changes and detect the potential of deception. Once they put the doubt on you, and not on themselves, it would be very hard to perform any manipulative or deceptive techniques on your target. Should that happen, you would need to make sure that you prove your trustworthiness by telling them a number of true reasons why you should be trusted and suggest he question himself for feeling it necessary to doubt you. When you are able to pull that off, you successfully planted self-doubt, which is key to this technique. However, you need to watch your step – it does not mean that when the target doubts himself, he has no reason to doubt you, too.

Chapter 25. How to Make People Always Say Yes

When you are manipulating people into doing what you want, you might wonder if they are going to say, “yes” to you the next time you ask them to do something which is to your benefit. According to psychologists, there is a big chance that they would, if you manage to make sure that you lead them right into that situation. The techniques that often work to achieve this condition are called the Foot in the Door (FITD) and the Door in the Face (DITF) tactics.

These tactics are used to make sure that you get compliance from your target without pressure, which is a great skill that manipulators have. The use of pressure makes your target feels that you are trying to bait him into doing something that he does not want to do, which makes him build walls and reject you the second he gets the opportunity. For this reason, these tactics are designed to make your target feel he has freedom to say “yes” or “no” to any of your requests, which makes him feel empowered and safe. After all, he knows that he can just close the door when he knows that he does not like what you are saying.

However you, the manipulator, know how to take advantage of that false sense of security that you provided through the way you presented your requests. Through asking favors, you will realize that it is possible to make someone want to do you favors because he has the freedom to of choosing to. You will even experience your targets too willing to do you a favor without even asking them, because they feel that they have the means to do so. Now, that is manipulation without any effort at all!

What is the Foot-in-the-Door technique?

You might hear the term used by people who are saying that they have a big chance in getting what they want, because they already have a form of leverage that makes the door of opportunity open for them, hence the phrase "foot in the door." For manipulators, these is a phenomenon that happens when they manage to create successive requests with successive and positive results, which makes them able to make larger requests and still get the result that they want.

For example, you are likely to say "No" if a stranger calls you and then asks you if they can come over and look at the stuff that you are storing in your garage. You would definitely find this request extremely strange, and you would think that this person is simply asking for too much, to the point that you have to go out of the way and do something that you simply do not want to do. However, if that stranger is a good manipulator, he can increase the likelihood that you will say "yes" to his request, no matter how absurd it is because manipulators make you feel that you want to help.

There was an experiment conducted in 1966 where two researchers from Stanford called four groups of housewives who were alone in their homes during weekdays. The three groups were asked to answer some questions about some kitchen products that they normally use. After three days, they were contacted again and then asked if some stranger can visit them at the house and catalog all the items that they have in their kitchen. The fourth group was asked the second request, and not the first one.

The fourth group in this experiment reacted the way any person should – they did not agree to have someone come over to their house and see the contents of their kitchen cabinets. They saw no reason to. However, about 53% of the respondents from the three groups that agreed to answer the survey also said "yes" to the second request. For this reason, the research concluded that once you manage to make someone do you a favor, there is a higher possibility that you are going to get them to do you another favor the next time you ask them. At the same time, you can also make them fulfill a much more difficult request that may be totally unrelated to the first request that you asked them to do. They may feel anxious to do it, but they are still likely to say "yes" to you.

Why FITD Works

This technique has been a great tool in ensuring compliance for a number of community-based requests, such as asking for donations, putting a sign in people's cars to remind others to drive carefully, or to exercise their right to vote during elections. The reason why it works for these campaigns is that it gives the person the sense of responsibility while making them feel that they are doing something useful of their own free will.

The other reason is that people will always have a strong sense of community, and they also like to build relationships with the people that they meet. You will realize that whenever you make donations, you tend to fill up a survey or a registration form, which strengthens your bond with the organizer. Since you feel that you have become familiar and connected to him in some way, you are willing to do something else for him, even though that means giving away your money. But hey, it is for a cause that you know you supported. You already expressed your support the moment you filled up the form previously and that leads them to being able to ask for more. You will also notice that you are more willing to donate when the organizer mentions that you can refuse if you do not want to, because you have a choice. Ironic as it seems, you tend to lose your freedom to decide when you are reminded that you can freely choose what to do. However, since you are more aware of the environment that you are volunteering into, you feel that it is okay to do that person or charity a favor.

The Elements of FITD

Based on the examples above, you will notice that in order to perform the FITD technique successfully, you have to consider the following factors:

1. The target's awareness of the nature of the favor

2. The relationship that you want to build with your target

3. The ability of the target to fulfill the next favor/s

When you want to perform this tactic, it is very important that you have a tool to make the other person become attached to the nature of the favor that you want him to do for you. Notice how real estate agents get the attention of potential buyers? They ask them to simply accept the pamphlet that they are handing out. They are not forcing them to buy – they are merely just handing out really harmless materials, without asking them if they need a new house. Now that initial contact is very important. It allows the agent to move on to the second stage – the target realizes that the agent is just trying to do his job, and there is no harm in helping him out by getting the flyer. Then, the agent proceeds by asking questions, which is actually creating a rapport. Then, he asks for the target's phone number. Of course, this sequence of favors is targeted to make him go into that final favor of asking the target to buy a new house from him.

Looking at this example, you need to create the notion that this person is doing you a favor, and it is an easy one that would not harm his resources. You build the sequence of favors to build your relationship – it is as if you are getting him into the momentum of just saying "yes", and you trick him into thinking that all the requests that you are trying to make are easy. Space these favors strategically to make him forget the levels of difficulty in performing the tasks that you made him do. Then, have him perform the task that you really want him to do.

Now, it is very important that you take into consideration the ability of your target to fulfill the task. It should be reasonable and it should seem easy for him to do. You cannot ask a man who is strapped for cash to buy a car from you right away. You can instead build up on how he can easily get a loan, and if he can do that for you. Remember that in order for your target to think that the requests are reasonable, offer him easy solutions when you think that it is hard for him to perform the next favor. That way, all your favors are reasonably easy and your target will usually be happy say yes to your requests and perform them.

When FITD Does Not Work

At some point, people realize that they are being led on to doing something that they are unsure of. If you are trying to sell them a phone and then they do not wish to answer a questionnaire or get a pamphlet, then you might not be able to get them to buy anything from you. At this point, you need to reconsider your tactics.

When FITD does not work, you can do yet another technique, which is the Door in the Face technique. DITF works as the reverse of FITD – instead of trying to build rapport and lessen the anxiety of your target in order for him to comply with a series of requests for you, you can make him do one request for you by working on something outside of his anxiety level.

How DITF Works

People do not always trust others, but it does not mean that they are not willing to work with them. The distrust, or the idea that what you are asking them to do is uncomfortable, may lead them to doing you one reasonable favor so you can get your foot out of the door.

Remember the example mentioned about the housewives? If the fourth group refuses to have someone catalog all the contents of their kitchen cabinets, then what would they say about having to answer a questionnaire about kitchen products? You are likely to think that they would most likely agree to that, because it is more reasonable and much easier to do. If the researcher's goal is to really collect survey content from different housewives, then he was still able to get what he wants by changing his question. The point is that the person confronted with the question just wants it over and done with so that they can close the door on the problem, so is likely to comply with smaller requests, which do not touch their anxiety levels.

The main element of DITF is the anxiety of the target to get rid of the manipulator, but since they are also trying to establish a positive relationship with one another, both the target and the manipulator would assume that they want to give each other a favor. The target, being unable to comply with the first request, would say yes to the second one. The manipulator, on the other hand, would be doing his target a favor by removing the anxiety he caused with the first request that he made.

With that said, there are two factors that you need to consider when you use the DITF tactic:

1. A very reasonable first request, which your target has the means to fulfill, yet would possibly not want to, due to anxiety levels

2. A more reasonable and easier second request, which is very likely to be fulfilled by your target.

Why is the target still willing to do you a favor? It has to do with their sense of guilt – when requests are very reasonable and they are within their means, anyone would feel guilty for not wanting to fulfill them. This guilt builds up as anxiety the more you press the target to do something, telling him that he has the option of doing or not doing the task, even though he is a perfect candidate for fulfilling it. This reasoning is also present in the FITD system, but instead of granting the target the fulfillment of establishing a good mutual relationship with you, you take advantage of his hesitation instead as a means to help you out. You build up on the things that he can do but he chooses not to. That would cause the anxiety that you want to be caused, and you do that without having to lie.

This is the reason why most people are willing to donate to a cause, instead of having to go out there and become a volunteer. Both tasks are reasonably easy, and fulfilling them provides the reward of becoming a better citizen and performing the obligation of helping out the needy. However, not everyone would be willing to do the nitty-gritty tasks of organizing food caravans or building livelihood projects from scratch. They think that those things are too difficult and they do not have the patience or perhaps even the skills to fulfill them. It is much easier for them to dig into their pocketbooks and shell out a donation. The moment they give the money, they feel alleviated of their guilt, and at the same time, they receive the reward of being able to fulfill their social obligation. It becomes a reverse psychology tactic that works for both parties.

It's All about Probability

When you are considering what kind of tactic would have better applied for a given situation, you also would need to put yourself in the shoes of the target. If you were in his situation, which of the requests makes more sense? Which is more rewarding?

At this point, you would need to go back to the very idea of building rapport and the idea of how to sell an idea to your target. Anyone wants to experience rewards out of their actions, but the idea of what a reward is would depend on the profile of the target. You might remember that visual people find things that they see being accomplished to be more rewarding, than those who hear reports about them or are presented with verbal facts. You will realize that identifying the buying types of people would make you see what kinds of favors they are more willing to do.

By profiling the targets that you meet and recognizing their style straight away, you make sure that you get the idea of how probable your requests are, depending on the person that you are dealing with. You would expect visual people to volunteer and make the FITD tactic work better and make them progress to doing harder tasks, simply because they want to see progress for themselves. You would, however, expect auditory people to make donations because they are likely to be content with hearing progress from other people. To increase the probability that they are going to make a donation, you can use the DITF tactic.

The more you make use of this tactic, the easier it becomes for you to profile people according to the tasks that they are willing to do. Of course, make sure that you can easily provide evidence that they can fulfill the requests that you are asking them to increase the likelihood of getting them to agree with you. Providing the evidence that it does not take much effort for them to do the tasks that they are asked to do should become second nature to you, especially if you want to increase the frequency of using either FITD or DITF manipulation techniques. The evidence that you present would serve as your counter-argument to any hesitation that they would show. With that in mind, you can increase the number of requests that you can get done, without having to use force on your targets.

This is done all the time with advertising and the message that people can do things and that they are within their reach mean that they are more likely to comply. Watch the TV ads closely and you will see this technique being demonstrated over and over again.

Chapter 26. Make Them Buy Something Else

One of the greatest skills of salesmen is to sell all the items that they have in their inventory and make sure that customers find them appealing and proceed to buy more. Most of the time, they do it by advertising a product and when customers want to buy it, they sell another product instead, particularly a product that is more expensive or that item in the inventory that they most want to get rid of. Most people, especially consumer rights advocates, call this the bait and switch.

Bait and Switch Explained

Bait and switch happens when you do the following:

1. Make an offer that is incredibly valuable to your target that is so attractive it is impossible for him not to buy it.

2. When your target proceeds to take up the offer, offer him something else that has lower value to him, or something that makes you more profit.

When you look at how this trick works, it creates a scenario wherein you make more money by making that intention look like you are willing to lose some profit just to make a good deal with customers. However, there is a certain risk when it comes to performing this practice, which includes the danger of being sued for false advertising. For this reason, it is very important that you understand the nature of this tactic, when it is illegal and how to devise a workaround, and who the best candidates for this technique are.

Who Your Target Should Be

The best candidates for targets are those that are looking to save money, and when they see that the item that they love is in a clearance sale, they are likely to rush to the store without even thinking about the sincerity of the ad. They do not realize that there is no reason for merchants to drop prices at the drop of a hat, unless they do need to move their inventory. Also, most consumers who want to take advantage of a huge sale neglect to read the fine print, and even when disclosures such as limited availability or a deadline on the sale are made, they go ahead anyway because they believe that they may gain something. Most of the time, they end up buying the product at its original price, or buying another product that may not even look like the original item that they intended to buy.

This tactic works because of the state of mind that you put your targets through. You make them crave for an item and make them believe that they are going to get it. You may offer a coupon that allows them to dine in a very expensive restaurant that all the bloggers in the world have been raving about. Of course, since it is a top-rated restaurant, it is very possible that it is fully booked and they cannot get in to have a seat. The very idea that they are so close to getting what they want and then being refused by the manipulator puts them into great anxiety. Of course, every person in the world wants to relieve themselves of that anxiety by taking the option available in order for them to still get something out of the situation.

Why do people behave this way then? You may observe that it looks the same as the Foot in the Door tactic (discussed in the previous chapter), which provides a lure to potential targets. It is always the case that when you are making an offer to a target, you go into a relationship which is based on you making an offer and your target taking it. You strengthen that bond by making an offer that is very important to the target so that even when he is not thinking about it, he still knows that it is valuable. When you take away that lure and then proceed to offer something else, the sense of obligation of your target to you is still there. You increase the likelihood of getting a "Yes" to your second offer because you already made it a point that your target would go to you to receive the initial offer, even though it's no longer available. Meanwhile, he can take the second offer instead and then come back later when he can take advantage of the more attractive offer. Wash, rinse, and repeat.

Shops do this regularly with drastic sales. People's expectations are built up and what happens is that when they are disappointed, they spend on other items to get rid of that disappointed feeling.

It is really simple to do, but of course, you may risk the target doubting you as an honest salesperson because of the inconsistency with the ad and reality. No one would really want to go to a store to buy a nice item, and then be pushed into buying something else. When your target feels that he is being downright cheated, you may both end up in a losing situation – you losing the chance to profit, him not getting anything that he wants.

Here's one thing that you need to know about doing bait and switch – there are clauses in the law of some countries that actually prohibit you from doing this. If you belong in a country not covered by this law, you still would tarnish your reputation and fail to be a foolproof manipulator. For this reason, it is very important for you to know what it is and how you can turn a bait and switch a situation into something else. What this means is that in order for you to avoid trouble, you need to learn the concept and avoid some of the common practices that make it look dishonest.

The Obvious Bait and Switch

Customers know that they are being targeted for a bait and switch tactic when they experience the following:

1. The salesperson tells them that there is something wrong with the "bait" and proceeds to disparage its quality or warranty.

2. They are being shown a defective product.

3. They are told that the product is on the backorder and would ship outside reasonable time so is not viable.

4. The store knows the demand for the product but they did not tell potential customers anything about possible limitation or quantity in the ad.

5. The salesperson refuses to take their order, telling a customer that he would be penalized if he sold the last item on display.

6. The advertisement offers something that is too good to be true, with confusing deal terms that are often considered final.

When you are going to give these excuses to your targets, it is easy to suspect that you are baiting them for a switch, which could put you in serious trouble later on. The goal is for you to make money and not get bad reviews for your services. In order for you to avoid anything that would discredit you and still steer your customers away from bad experience and buyer's remorse, keep in mind that you need to avoid these scenarios. Sure, you are still going to lie about availability and quality, but you need to think of a better and undetectable lie. At the end of the day, you do not want to look like a seller with empty promises.

Remember that what upsets targets most, and prompts them to build walls around themselves, is the feeling that they are not getting anything out of their effort. Failure to relieve that anxiety that they felt when they realized that they are not getting the initial offer would lead them to barraging you with questions that you cannot get away from. At the same time, they will likely conclude that you merely baited them, or that you are just giving them a disappointing experience. The problem with this is that it makes them ready to complain.

However, you can take advantage of the situation by making use of it as another opportunity to offer them something that they would like. Keep in mind that most buyers do not really rationalize according to their needs, but rather, make decisions that are based on making them go back to their comfort zone. They know that they need to buy something in order for them to feel satisfied. They also feel that they need to achieve that target no matter what, even if they have to spend extra. This is where you make another offer that fills that need.

A Better Solution

What you need to do in order to make a successful bait and switch is to give another offer that may be much more expensive, but can still be sold as useful to your target. You do not want to expose yourself as a cheat, so make sure that you create another offer on the spot that looks like the offer that they want to take.

For example, if your customer wants to buy a laptop from your store because of the ad that you placed and then you want him to buy a more expensive and better available unit, think of something that would make him attracted to the model that you want to sell without destroying the reputation of the original product that he wants to get. This immediately puts you in the light that you have the ability to "sell" the advertised product, it's just that you are concerned about it being the right product for your customer's needs. Now, when you look at it, you can easily say that you just want to offer quality customer service.

Ask your target what he wants to use the laptop for, and then think of ways how the laptop that you want to offer does better work. You can compare the two products, but refrain from saying that the advertised product is not available. Your target obviously sees the display, and would push toward buying it even if it is the last unit. When you deny its existence, you are going to be pushed to lie and go through all the excuses that bad bait and switch practitioners go through, and then expose yourself as inconsistent and completely dishonest.

If your target wants a laptop that is for gaming, typing, surfing, or just to watch movies from, you simply have to say that the laptop that you are offering will be able to help him do all the jobs that he has specified efficiently. Throw in a free mouse or a headphone or anything that would not hurt your inventory to make your new offer more attractive than the lure. When you upsell another product, you are not saying anything bad about the initial ad – you are simply offering a product that would make much more sense to your target.

When you upsell another product, albeit being more costly to your target, you are not breaking the consistency between your relationship. You are trying to make it look like the offer has improved, and you are trying to make your target realize that you are the expert when it comes to understanding his needs. That way, you are still trying to make both parties meet their obligations. The more expensive laptop may actually have better speakers, a better sound card, and a better graphics card. You can use any description as long as the customer sees you are trying to help him avoid making a mistake.

How to Get Away with the "Bait"

There are many people who write consumer reviews that announce that some practices of certain establishments are somewhat shady. However, you should make it a point that you observe guidelines that would make your practice fall under bait and switch. For this reason, take advantage of the following factors that helps you get away with the bait and then make the most out of your lure:

1. When you talk to your target about buying something else and not the bait that is not "bait and switch," but merely an upsell. Of course, you have to tell your target that you do have the ability to sell the product that they intend to buy if they still want it.

2. When you tell your target that you ran out of the "bait" but you made it a point to inform them that you are selling this product in limited quantities, and then you get away with the bait and switch.

These two factors make your practice legal, even when you really are intending to just bait your targets and make them another offer, and it actually strengthens the appeal of your bait and then makes your targets look at other goods. They also feel confident that your advertisement can be take advantage of at another time, and they continue to trust you because you did not bait them with an outright lie and then try to wiggle out of inconsistently. They can see the product is all right; it's just that from what you are telling them there are better options. If you did "run out" of the advertised product, you already told them that they should have arrived earlier, but it is not too late to buy a product that they need, but of course, not at the same discount.

When you want to get away with a bait and switch tactic without looking shady, make it a point that you are still doing your target a favor. You can do this by turning the table around and then pointing out that it is not the availability of the product that has a problem here – it is the customer. This way, you can tell the target that you could have done a better service and could have provided him the very thing that he wants if he only arrived early. However, it is a shame to have come all this way to go away empty-handed when other products meet his specs.

Again, it is not the establishment's fault that he was not able to get it, but you are trying to go out of your way to find something else in your store that would fit his needs. To apologize for the inconvenience that he had to drive a long way or go online and realize that the product is out of stock, you are going to throw in some freebies and see if you can give a discount on the new item. You are trying, and the customer can always detect when a salesperson is going through some inconvenience just to help him out. That inconvenience strengthens the customer's obligation to buy, and he is now itching to make it easier for you. It is even possible that he would buy the new product now without any discount or freebies. You just need to throw them in to promote you as a provider of good service.

Should You Rely on Bait and Switch?

Seeing the risk and the sensitivity of the bait and switch may make you feel that it is not a tactic that you can use a lot of the time. However, you can take advantage of this technique by matching it with other techniques such as the foot in the door to maximize its impact. You can use the bait and switch tactic to lure your target, and then perform FITD to increase the number of requests that you can have your target comply with. When you do that, you can increase the profit that you can make in any day to more than any traditional sellers would achieve.

Bait and switch becomes a great tactic when you know that you have two or more products or services that you can offer, and you have understanding of what your target wants. You can also come out of a situation like this making your target think you are exceptionally helpful, because you told them the drawbacks of the other cheap item for his use and have come up with a better long term solution, even if it is a little more expensive. It would only work if you are certain that you have good bait, and that involves understanding of what your target really wants and having the ability to get it into his hands. When you do, you have the perfect opportunity to create a bait and switch situation, because you do have the item that they want and that satisfies his need to buy.

Chapter 27. Practical Hacks on How to Keep Customers Shopping

If you have a business and you want to sell more, then you need to know more about the covert tactics that you have been dealing with every day. You may not know it, but every shop that you have been into is making a lot of money because of certain tricks that are designed into making you buy and respond to their offers positively.

Most of the activities that customers can do inside a shop can be manipulated to play an active role of a merchant's marketing ploys. The design of packaging, the number of steps or clicks that you need to make, pricing, timing, and even placement of basic amenities such as bathrooms and customer service booths all add up to making consumers buy more than they expect.

If you want to use the same tactics in your business establishment or prep your online store to be extra profitable, you have to understand that these manipulation techniques do not work well on their own, but when added together, can make massive impact. Establishments that sell are normally designed to manipulate every movement and each design piece is in coordination with others, making them very effective when it comes to selling. Of course, it also comes to mind that every person can be convinced by appealing to their sense of comfort and anxiety. You can easily deduce that every marketing ploy present in all business establishments is designed to press on the idea of comfort and stress levels of each potential customer.

Placement Matters

When you enter a grocery or enter an online shop, you may have a couple of items in your mind that you intend to buy.

However, no matter what you do, you always end up at the checkout counter paying for more items than you initially had in mind. Why does this happen every time you shop? The reason is that the moment you set your eyes on the shop, you are already being tricked into buying more than you should.

If you are going to build a shop and you want your customers to do the same thing, keep in mind that the design of your establishment can dictate the quantity of the items that they buy. Add some services that would make buying a hassle-free experience, and you have the guarantee that you are going to be a rich man sometime soon. Here are some design elements that will be sure to help you achieve those extra sales.

1. Shopping carts

No shopping cart is designed to contain a limited number of items, and they are always placed in such a way that they are the first things that you see when you enter a shop, whether it is online or a bricks-and-mortar shop. You will also notice that attendants in a store are often on hand to hand you a basket or a shopping cart the moment that you pick up the first item on your list. You would not need a basket to carry that, but it is handed to you anyway, so you might as well use it.

When you give someone a basket or a shopping cart, you are already sending the message that they are there to shop and to fill up that container that you just gave them. When it gets full, you can simply hand them another one or you direct them to where the bigger carts are. Of course, the logic that would follow is that as long as they do not feel that the cart is full, they believe that they are not buying that much.

2. Profitable layout

Yes, there is such a thing as a profitable layout, and that means that you can instantly upsell items depending on how far or near they are from the entrance and the checkout counter. Look at department stores and how they see to it that you will pass through cosmetics and pricey apparel before you reach the commodities that you need, such as socks and underwear. Groceries also feature this kind of layout, where you first see the expensive items before you reach the basic goods, such as sugar and eggs, which are usually at the end of the store. The reason is simple – exposure to the items that can be marked up increases the likelihood that you are going to place them in your cart before you buy the essentials. Online stores also apply this by making the most expensive product appear on the homepage and making it a little harder to search for basic commodities or clearance sales. You do know that there is a sale in there, but the site is designed to make you look at the very attractive yet expensive item first.

3. The use of senses

It is traditional for shops to lure their customers into different areas using different senses. You have free taste promos in the grocery not for you to just try out the new seasoning but to also look at the prepared meals at the store. You will also feel the need to buy new cologne when you see the perfume salesmen with their sleek look. You would also think that you are hungry when you smell freshly baked bread near the entrance. Of course, you will feel thirsty after walking around that vast mall and that is why they have the more expensive drinks near the checkout counters for your convenience. Accompanying the drinks are more expensive, yet delicious chocolates that you can't resist. With stores taking advantage of the impulse-oriented products in every corner, it becomes impossible for the customer not to buy.

Even at the cash desk, there are last minute treats to be had that are slipped into the basket at the last moment.

4. Eye level

You will notice that items are arranged in such a way that the more expensive ones are at your eye level while the cheaper ones, the ones that you are searching for, are placed in the bottom racks. While some of the price conscious customers would not mind kneeling to retrieve the items that they do want to buy, a lot of consumers would simply put the item that they can easily see and reach into the shopping cart. They don't want the hassle of kneeling down.

These are common tactics that simply make use of how things inside the store are arranged. They do look innocent, but how items are arranged inside any store provides leverage over the most discerning customer that would enter the establishment. The reason is simple – everybody shops because of convenience. The more convenient it is to get an item, the more likely that item is going to be sold. While this may be deception to you, it qualifies as a means to upsell the products that make a lot of profit by simply presenting them first and making it easily possible for you to carry them to the counter.

Deception happens on an entirely different level. Any shop owner knows that it is possible to trick a person into thinking that they are really on their way to savings and convenience by making pricing and packaging appear differently.

5. The number of stops

The most profitable shops take advantage of the turns and aisles inside their shop in order for them to make the most out of their product placement. These shops make it a point that their customers make necessary stops – the more they stop walking, the more items are placed inside the carts.

You may notice that there are too many distractions inside a store, even the online ones, as if you are navigating through a maze of advertisements before you reach the products that you really want to buy. The more confused a target customer is when it comes to where he should be going, then the more prone he is to falling for advertising ploys.

The Magic of Design, Texts, and Packaging

You probably know by now that how a product is presented matters when it comes to making a lot of profit. You may be the type of buyer that would typically get an item when it is handy and stylish. However, do you know that how a product is wrapped in a box and captioned in the store is actually designed to make you tempted by them, no matter how much it costs?

Steve Jobs, one of the most brilliant marketers that you probably know, made a lot of emphasis on these advertising concepts. He believes that should you ever need to make an important note in any selling concept, you have to make sure that it is written in big letters. By big, he meant huge. He knows that people tend not to notice the smaller fonts and if it is smaller, then feel it is less important. It is in the nature of every literate man in the world. At the same time, he knows that he can drill a concept and sell an idea by simply writing it using a large and attractive font.

Apart from that, you will also notice how he managed to make products look cooler and smarter than the rest, despite being able to perform the same tasks. Look at the iPhone and the iPod and compare them with Android and Blackberry phones and the Walkman. They are designed to do the same job, but because the Apple products look different and come in sleek-looking packaging, they managed to become extremely sellable despite a higher price. How did that happen?

Design, texts, and packaging make use of what the target's brain easily deduces and categorizes into common sense. Thanks to a person's experience, he is trained to think that large fonts convey the most important information, instead of realizing that it is a lure. An object that is placed inside a large box is easily thought of as a large object, but in reality, the target is merely paying for more air than goods. Sleek designs are also thought of as intuitive and game changing, even if the function of the product is just the same as the cheaper-priced ones. However, it takes a little more than that to convince the consumer who is biased toward a particular product.

The Idea of Packages, Limited Time and Quantity

Customers are always attracted to sales, and that is the reason why Black Friday and similar sale events are here to stay. However, if you know how business works, these events are actually designed to make people shell out more money than making actual savings. The secret of the success of these events is the presentation of bulk packages that take advantage of the season, the limited time a person can think about his purchase, and the limited quantity of the items that he can get. These concepts trigger the anxiety of the target to get more items that are advertised to be at a lower price, and of course, save him from the hassle of thinking too much about his purchases.

Putting all these selling techniques together, shops can manipulate their customers into doing the following:

1. Mindlessly placing items on carts

When pressured into being able to choose products for a limited time, targets are bound to not put too much attention on the products that they are placing into their cart. Most shops take this manipulation technique as leverage into pressuring their customers into buying something that they do not really need, and then pressuring them into making a purchase by adding a timer on the advertisement. If you see a trip to Haiti package that is sold for only $100 and you only have less than a minute to take it, you would only scan for the details that are most beneficial to you, especially if you want to take a vacation. Checking about the accommodation and other incentives would become an afterthought, and of course, it is too late to change your mind once you have paid.

2. Neglecting a price check

Most shops can easily trick a customer into thinking that he landed a great deal, but in reality, it is quite often the opposite. Customers do not think about making price checks and comparisons when they are being pressured into buying goods in a short period of time. When they see that the price is displayed in big bold letters, they automatically deduce that it is a sale price, not realizing that this has been the price of a product ever since it was sold in the store.

Sale items are also designed to display prices where it makes it hard to do the math for the targeted customers. While it is easy to think that a kilo pack of detergent worth $8 is worth more than a 500g detergent that is worth $5, shops can take advantage of the fact that their targets normally do the math by dividing the whole numbers and neglect what comes after the decimal point. They display the prices instead as $5.65, and then get two for $10.89. If you bought two items and you think that it is just the same because half of 10 is 5, then you made a mistake. Customers often do and retailers depend upon it to up the profits.

Another trick that shops do is manipulating their customer's minds into thinking that they are getting a better deal when they get packs of 10 instead of buying a single item. As a customer, you are getting the message clearly that normally, bundles of 10 sold for $10 each means that you are getting a huge discount for buying a bigger quantity. However, you might want to take a closer look at the price of the individual item. What manipulators do not want their customers to see (and often get away with) is that they really are offering each piece for a dollar and that's the normal price so the $10 bargain isn't such a bargain.

3. Neglecting to consider brand and quality

Here is one of the tactics that you may often see in big sales events such as the Black Friday – the shops give a forecast about the products and brands that are available, along with the price slash that they are willing to offer. When they open their stores for customers, they know that they do not have enough quantity of the advertised products, and they are aware that they are covered by the placement in their ad that these items are available in limited quantities. To make up for the demand, they offer a different brand with a similar product, and it may be poor quality. Again, this is a classic bait and switch strategy, but this works better for the store.

Their target customers, being pressured into buying the said products, do not realize that they are buying a different brand, which is offered for a much lower price. They may be lured into buying a TV from Pentax, without even realizing that the brand of the product that they just bought is actually great with film equipment, but not television. Because they have been satisfied with their ability to buy a new television for a lower price, they do not realize that they have been duped by the store into getting a product that they do not really have in mind.

4. Totally forgetting about their shopping list

Most customers try to be savvy and incorporate the use of shopping list in order for them to stick to buying what they need. However, the savvier shops make it a point to see to it that those lists become useless by offering package deals. When you think about it, package deals are designed for customers to be lured into buying more but paying less than the individual regular prices. They did save money on the one part, but they spent for items that they would not really need. Thus, they may end up having to throw away fresh items that they really can't use up in time.

Packages also target men and women who have kids or are thinking of buying gifts for numerous people, or those who are too lazy or busy to think about what they should be buying as gifts. Because they are lured with the idea that they can get more with less effort and at a cheaper price, they end up buying outside their normal needs as well.

Customers Will Still Love It

Even though a customer realizes that he has fallen for a trick, the mere idea of having purchased the product makes him defend his decision automatically. No customer, apart from the ones that have unknowingly purchased a defective product, would want to admit that he has purchased a product that is actually worth less than what he paid for it. It makes him look foolish.

Because he thought deeply about buying that product and was convinced of the advertisement, he seldom realizes that he can actually get more for less. The moment that a buyer receives a product and it functions the way he expected it to, price would not matter anymore to him. Because the product fulfills all the things that the ad promised, plus some incentives that would hardly make the product become more efficient or more reliable, he would think that there is nothing wrong about how the product was sold to him. All that matters is that he purchased an object that would alleviate his anxiety or fulfill a need. When he needed a phone or a bag of chips, he got it. End of story.

If you want to use these manipulating techniques, keep in mind that they will always work as long as you are able to get your customer's guard down. It is improbable for them to notice all the baits that you have laid out in your shop. Also remember that most of the tricks mentioned in this chapter are designed to go well together – some are even made to complement one trick for maximized impact, and may not work without the others.

For this reason, see to it that you are creating a business design that would incorporate all the tactics discussed. Once you do, you can guarantee yourself that you will never lose a day's sale in your shop again! Even on your online store, this can work in the same manner.

Chapter 28. Create the Best Persuasive Ad

A while back, you learned about the concepts of persuasion and manipulation. At this point, you also know that advertisements are usually created to adhere to the rules of psychological manipulation and direct a target audience into buying or doing something that they would probably not do without any outside influence.

If you are a businessman, you probably rely on advertisements a lot. Without them, you probably do not have any efficient means of reaching out to your audience and convincing them that you are the best provider of the products that you offer and they need to buy from you. However, are you sure that you are getting your message across? Are you sure that your campaigns are persuasive enough to make them flock to your business and help you make a profit?

Why Do Ads need to be Persuasive First (And Not Manipulative or Deceptive)

Advertisements exist to help you reach out to other people and let them know that you are offering something that they could find useful. At this point, you might realize that you cannot cater to the entire world. That means that by the time you picked up a product and intended to sell it, you know that you have a selected group of people in mind that would probably be your target audience. You advertise in order for more people to realize that they want your product, and that your intention is to give them what they want.

You might argue that you want to make more money, and during difficult times, you will want to have a more aggressive stance to get that profit, hence, you are willing to be manipulative. However, go back to the intentions of persuasion, manipulation, and deception. When you are running a business and you want these selected people to come back to your store, you have to think of the intent of the ad. Most of the time, an extra persuasive ad works better than those that intend to manipulate or deceive.

The main benefit of being persuasive is that you can maximize the benefit you can expect in an extended amount of time. Manipulation and deception works for a limited time, and they are often useful when you want a quick source of profit. You can push it to your targets and tweak their comfort zones in order for them to take actions that work in your favor, of course. However, manipulation and deceit mostly come with a price – once it is uncovered, or they make the target feel too uncomfortable and they back away because of it, you will definitely have difficulty tearing their wall of defenses down in the future, because they have realized that you are making them do something that it is not in their best interest. Most of the time, they would not want to offer you another invitation to sell them another idea. If you are selling something, you do not want any of your targets to feel that way, unless you really don't care about whether they come back or not.

Persuasion is Cooperation

What is it that you want your ad to achieve? You want your target audience to cooperate with you by buying your products, and let them think that it is a win/win situation. A win-win situation is something that manipulation and deceit would neglect to provide in the long run, because these tactics are discoverable and avoidable when your targets improve their learning curve. However, if you lure them with persuasion, this provides them with the confidence that they will:

1. Benefit from your offer

2. Be able to get a product that meets their expectation

3. Experience something that has an add-on value

When you are creating an ad, you have to satisfy these needs, and at the same time, create the belief that you are going to meet these demands with consistency. When you manage to incorporate these in your ad, you do not have to tell your target consumers that whatever offer you have is not a scam, because you have already established the idea that you are working with customers and have a reputation to uphold.

Enter Other Contexts

Now that you know what you want to offer, it's time to look at other factors that you also need to consider when you are creating an ad. Here's the problem that you would normally face – buyers do not know what they want and sometimes they let their emotions lead them to the products that they want and then randomly assign value to them. What can possibly make a person buy a pair of socks for $10? What kind of value do they get out of it, and don't they sense that they are being cheated out of their money? When you think about it, the company that sold them was able to produce another commodity through their ad, which is the emotional value of the product.

Putting emotional value, such as the sense of being important and successful, safe, beautiful, or outstanding, is not necessarily a form of manipulation. Advertisers and company owners know that more than simply adhering to practicality, consumers buy to fill emotional needs. The good news is that these needs are immediately promised to them by the images that they see and the copy that they read.

How to Steer Them in the Right Direction

Certain design concepts are widely used when it comes to directing people into their goals. For example, the use of colors has been very useful when it comes to advising customers about the values that certain brands uphold. Blue does not only tell customers that a brand is leaning towards creativity, it also makes them think that a brand is dependable. The color green tells that the brand that uses it promotes holistic and healthy approach, while white promotes simplicity and clean design. In one way or another, colors give customers this message: if you are living a particular kind of lifestyle, then you should buy brands that are packaged using a particular color.

Now, when you are making ads for any product or service that you are promoting, you do not necessarily sell the product and assume that your target does not have it yet. You show them what their life would be like if they had it already. You sell them the experience, and then tell them later how your product works. That way, they can immediately experience the value that you are offering BEFORE they even get the product.

What can you do in order to get your target to feel positively towards your ad, and end up as a buyer? Here are some things that you can do:

1. Write and show what is interesting to them.
Buyers do not really read and watch everything in an ad – they skim and find all elements that attract them. They do not want to know that Product X is created with fish oil. What they want to know is that it can increase their focus

and make them do their jobs better or that it has health benefits.

2. Explain the value in the clearest way possible.
If you are selling a toy and you can't explain to a 4th grader, why he would want to have it? There is no way that he could tell his parents that he wants that toy or how badly he wants it. For that reason, you need to make the value feel simple, yet very direct, because you are not sure who is going to see your ad. If it appeals to everyone, then you are sure that it will go a long way toward promoting the product and increasing sales.

3. Be consistent.
If you want to tell future customers that Product X is designed to improve their lives and make them rich, don't tell them that you are going to charge a lot for your service on your ad. Getting rich and paying a lot of money does not really go well together in one statement.

4. Tell a Story
People will always be emotional buyers and they do not really buy things that they do not need emotionally. They do not want to buy a brand of noodles because it is cheap – they want their dinner table to be a happier place by serving those noodles to their loved ones. Paint a scenario that they crave for emotionally.

Note: Being Persuasive Does Not Mean Telling Everything

When you are trying to offer someone help, and you are trying to get something in return, you sometimes feel obliged to justify your product with all the information you have. Telling your target customers everything will make you become more confident and credible, right?

No, it doesn't happen that way. Most people buy the instant that they hear what they need and then pace themselves into the scenario where they already experience a product or a service offered to them. Too much information, whether helpful or not, can destroy that image that you want customers to have on their minds. Remember advertising is short and so are the attention spans of potential customers.

Whether you are using an ad or not, the key to making someone buy something from you and make them think that it is worth the investment is simply telling them what they need to know. On many occasions, going beyond that actually tells them that they should back off from a deal. Think about the many situations where you stepped out of a shop because the salesperson is "too helpful." Being too helpful can prompt a person to think that there must be something that he is missing out on in the deal. That prompts your target to ask questions and raise defenses. That overly helpful sales assistant drives potential customers away. So will adverts that give too much detail.

Now that you know how to use persuasion and future pacing in order to make someone commit to your product even before they have experienced what you are offering them, it's time to go beyond sales. The next chapter will show you all the tricks you need to know to implant a very strong idea in your target's mind.

Chapter 29. The Art of Being Compelling

Most of the things that you have learned so far in this book target one goal, and that is to implant strong ideas in your target customer and make it stick in their minds as long as possible. The result of that goal, of course, is to create a belief in your target that will allow you to control him, and earn the benefit of doing so. In this chapter, you will learn how to see to it that all the ideas that you are going to create are compelling and when you tell your target about them, it is going to stick in his mind and perform an action that is favorable to you.

Planting the Idea

How do you create an unshakeable idea and plant it in your target's mind? For example, if you are concerned about a member of your family always eating a bucket of fried chicken during dinner, you might want to say directly that "Eating that much chicken is bad for you." Your target is likely to say that he knows it, and he would take it into consideration. Of course, you see him doing it again.

Everybody can easily resist an idea even when they know that it is right in front of them. However, if you say, "I heard that chickens are killing a million people in (insert name of obscure place here)." your target is likely to reconsider his actions. He would still think of doing it, but his mind would go "Is a chicken really capable of doing that?" Take note that you did not directly tell him to stop eating chicken, and you did not tell him about your entire plan. However, you made a strong suggestion that chicken can possibly be bad for him. Suggestion is a very powerful tool.

Talk Around the Concept

There was a show that Derren Brown, one of the best mind manipulators on television, created where he would attempt to guess what his target would write and draw on a piece of paper. You already have an idea that that entire plot is a trick – of course, he already knows what's going to be placed on the blank piece of paper. He did not deduct it – he merely placed subtle images in his target's mind and then predicted the most logical image that is going to be made out of them.

When you are making a person think in a particular way, you also have to take note of all the things that are going on within your target's environment. Take note that all the things that a person believes in – how he crafts his belief in his religion, what he thinks about money, and all other founded knowledge that he adheres to – are all because of his experiences. The mind takes in all the things that the senses perceives and then craftily arranges them in such a way whereby they make sense. It does not matter if all the things that a person experiences are true or not – the mind makes sense of it and then creates an image that is worth believing in.

Going back to the example of your loved one with the bad habit of eating chicken, how did he possibly get the idea that chickens are delicious, especially when served in a bucket with lots of gravy and mashed potato? That's right – he got it from advertising. You know that there are just too many billboards, TV commercials and shows that tell people how great fried chicken is. They do not really tell their targets, like your family member, how bad it can be for them. They just implant a strong idea thanks to all the images that they are able to provide around their targets.

Now, to counter that belief is easy. All you need to do is to do the same thing that ads do – make the image of fried chicken being bad for him available as well. Whenever you see a bird, talk about bird flu and how chickens can acquire it. Whenever you see a fried chicken piece, push it away from you. Watch a documentary about how sickly chickens can be before they get slaughtered and turned into fried goods. Have pamphlets telling about the dangers of GMO-fed poultry spread around your house.

Take Away the Absurdity

After exposing your family member to a number of images that would plant the idea that eating chickens are bad for him, he would probably still want to eat chicken, but have an extreme amount of doubt in his mind. You do not even have to prove your belief that what he is doing is bad for himself. You have already won the debate by making him doubt his actions.

To tie up loose ends, you would need to take away the absurdity. Of course he would find out sooner or later that he is scaring himself outside of his comfort zone over a belief that he can easily debunk with a simple Google search, and then you lose credibility. The sensible goal that you are trying to achieve is to make him consume fried chicken in moderation.

Now, tell your family member that you heard that fried chicken is not deadly as long as it is consumed in minimal amounts, say a single or two pieces every two days.

When you offer that belief, again, do not argue about it. Just set it down on the table for him to mull over. He knows that he is undergoing too much stress because he is doubting his chicken consumption, and he wants to get rid of that anxiety. By offering a sensible and very appealing solution to his problem, he would want to stick to the belief that you just presented to him. A piece or two of chicken is not as bad as having to eat no fried chicken at all.

Elements of a Compelling Concept

At this point, you would realize that in order to make a compelling belief that any target would stick to, you have to create a scenario that has the following elements:

1. A core belief, which you will not disclose to your target

2. A false belief and a set of evidences that supports it

3. A rewarding belief that your target would want to stick to

These elements, while looking like they are all beliefs that are unrelated to each other, would actually refer to the goal that you have in mind. You simply need to recreate the reality of a concept for your target and make it appear like a real human experience. Human beliefs all start from a broad concept, and then they become shaped according to what appeals the most to people. Of course, it differs from one person to another. However, by carefully studying a person's pressure point (what causes anxiety and what would create relief), pressing on it and making the pressure compelling by providing evidence, and then revealing the most beneficial form of the belief that you are trying to instill, you can create a belief that will have a permanent impact.

How does that happen? By making use of anxiety, and making it appear that the worst possible case can happen, your target will want to adhere to the alternative that you are going to present. He would find that that is the best way for him to go back to his comfort zone and save himself from possible pain. Because it is rewarding, he would want to take it above any other choices that he has in the scenario that you just painted.

Chapter 30. The Art of Influencing and Persuading

Influencing is offering someone something valuable to him or her. Something of value is something that the other person wants, needs or is committed to. It is equally important to have the opportunity to demonstrate that particular value.

To influence someone means to offer a solution to a problem or a need. It involves helping or offering means of working through any of the perceive barriers to achieve the desired outcome or obtain a goal, need or want.

Influencing is at the core of negotiation, solving problems, working with others, change and leading others.

Influencing skills

To fully develop effective influencing skills, you should be able to:

- Recognize, adequately respond to and target the different types of communication
- Gain an understanding of psychological processes involved in persuasion, which determines a person's willingness and tendency to be influenced
- Develop simple strategies in influencing others and have the opportunity and ability to carry out these strategies

How to be more persuasive when speaking

It isn't just the words you say that persuade other people. How you say them and your behavior while you speak play important roles, too.

Use eye contact when talking with someone. This gets their attention - and keeps it on you. It also makes them feel as if you are really connecting with them, especially if you are talking to an audience. Looking into their eyes also creates more intensity and sincerity.

Create variety by observing the changes in your tone, loudness of your voice, facial expressions and body language. Appearing monotonous makes you look too rehearsed and as a result, less sincere. It also makes you look unenthusiastic. You can't inspire people if you look uninspired yourself. When you do create variety, make sure that these are consistent with what you are saying. For example, if you are saying something happy, smile and talk in a happy, upbeat tone. If the content is sad, don't smile. Also, keep your body movements limited. While these can help make the concept more dynamic, a lot of moving around can make your audience seasick. They'd be too distracted with your movements. Stand straight with your shoulders back and your head up. This way, you appear more confident (even if you are not). When you talk, make an effort to sound sincere. Sound as if you really care about something. Creating variety also includes the words you use. Try to use synonyms instead of using the same words the entire time. For example, do not use "bad", "good", "beneficial", "revolutionary", etc. over and over. You won't be effective this way. Try to limit the use of keywords of your presentation. For example, if you are banking on your product as "revolutionary" or on the "new and experimental" method you want others to try, limit the use of these words.

Use examples and analogies to make your point more understandable and relatable. This will help create a sharper and more concrete image in your audience. Make sure, though, that you use appropriate ones. For example, use common adult experiences when talking to a group of adults, examples from the youth culture when talking to teenagers, etc.

Use strong openings to grab attention. Create a good and powerful impression at the beginning, and then, maintain it. This would require planning and practice to get the best and the most appropriate opening lines. It must match your audience too, in order to be effective.

Relationship-based Persuasive Techniques

This technique follows a 4-step process that is distinct from each other and repeatable.

Step 1 – Surveying the situation

This is a very important step before you even start persuading someone. You have to determine your ideas and goals. You should also consider the possible organizational challenges you might face. What idea, service, products, etc. are you trying to sell? What is distinctive about it? Also consider how you will communicate these ideas in each of your encounters. Assess yourself and determine to what extent are your committed to the idea. By doing so, you know where you stand, where you want to go, how to get there and how much you want to achieve these goals.

Step 2 – Confronting the 5 Barriers

The second step requires you to consider the hindrances you might encounter during your persuasion encounters. Think of possible obstacles and the degree to which these can thwart your efforts for successful persuasion. The barriers include relationships that are ambiguous or negative, poor credibility, mismatch in communication, belief systems that are hostile, and interests that are conflicting. Relationships and credibility are barriers related to how other people personally see you. Communication, belief systems and interests make it more difficult for other people to hear the ideas you present clearly. All of these barriers, if taken in the right context, can be used to support your persuasion endeavors.

Potential Barrier 1- Relationships

Persuasion always happens within a relationship network. Your starting point in presenting your idea is the kind of relationship you have with someone. Relationships you establish are also the end point of your persuasion efforts, which determines if you succeed or fail.

You need to have a circle of influence. This will be your core group, where you concentrate your efforts. Once persuaded, they will also persuade other people they know. However, this may not be possible if you need to sell an idea, product, service, etc. immediately. This requires you to form quick relationships. You should grab people's attention, establish rapport and maintain a good relationship throughout your persuasion encounter.

The biggest barrier to persuasion is when you have a hostile or negative relationship with someone. If the person you are trying to persuade does not like you or does not believe in the things you say, then, this relationship is an obstacle to your efforts. You should do something to ease that tension and dislike by using other techniques such as framing. Present your ideas in a way that is less offensive and more acceptable to the other person. This does not mean abandoning your idea. It is all about the manner of presentation.

Potential Barrier 2 – Credibility

Consider how others may see you. Do they see you as a credible source of information? Are you a credible advocate for the idea? For example, will people likely believe you when you talk about weight loss? This is where the results of Step #1 become very useful. If you are obese and you talk about the need and the benefits of weight loss, will people believe you? Chances are, no. People are likely to believe an advocate if they already see the results. You will be more credible if you are living proof of the idea you are pushing for.

Potential Barrier 3 – Mismatch in Communication

The 3rd potential barrier is the preferred communication style of your audience. You have to adjust your style in relation to the audience you will deal with. When communicating with your potential market, a naturally upbeat, enthusiastic and humorous communication style can be very effective. However, this same style is less likely to work when you are pitching ideas to an executive committee or to a group of somber potential investors. Adjust accordingly. You don't have to totally change your style. Sometimes, all you have to do is temper some aspects. For example, lessen the humor, speak more seriously (but not in a boring way) and smile less often when talking in the conference room. Speak in an upbeat tone and smile more often when outside, talking to customers.

Potential Barrier 4 – Belief systems

If your idea goes against the other person's core beliefs and values, it won't sell. People hold onto their belief systems. Anything that attacks their beliefs will make them feel uncomfortable and disconcerted. This can either be an advantage or disadvantage to you. You can attack their belief system and persuade them to change, in the manner you are advocating. For example, some obese people believe that they do not have to change their lifestyle because they are fine with what they are and what they have. You attack this belief by presenting the negative effects of their unhealthy lifestyle. They will be initially uncomfortable. As you narrate the risks they are putting themselves through, you are instilling concern and fear in their minds. After you have shaken their belief, you are more successful in persuading them to follow the healthy lifestyle/medication/weight loss regimen/etc. that you are advocating.

Attacking another person's beliefs may also be to your disadvantage. For instance, persuading people to use contraceptives will be rejected if these people believe in the value of family and sanctity of life.

In general, people tend to reject any of your ideas because it is easier for them to reject than to accept. People have a tendency to reject change. To increase your chances at successful persuasion, structure your ideas so that these will seem as if you are supporting and furthering the values and beliefs of your audience.

Potential Barrier 5 – Needs and Interests

The needs and interests of your audience, the target of persuasion efforts, can be to your advantage or can be a barrier. If your ideas do not appeal to the interests of your audience, they will be rejected. If they are in line with their interests and needs, then you will succeed in persuading them to behave, think or act the way you want. Take for example - Napoleon Bonaparte. He was one of the world's greatest persuaders. He persuaded his men to fight and cross deserts or icy terrains in all kinds of weather. He persuaded his soldiers to keep fighting and following him despite low provisions, ammunition and pitiful conditions. His secret? He knew how to motivate his people. He knew his soldiers' need to be known for their courage and he provided opportunities for his men to achieve this need.

By understanding what motivates people to act, behave and think, you have the tool to inspire, motivate, influence and persuade them. By focusing on their needs and interests, you get their attention and touch their emotions.

Needs and interests may, at times, be in conflict with the ideas you promote. Learn to adjust and decrease the tension between oppositions. This way, you develop and maintain positive relationships.

Step 3 – Making the pitch

Insights and understanding of the 5 potential barriers will help you in developing your presentation. These will help you gain a better perspective, which you will need in effectively framing your ideas.

This 3rd step involves the development of your pitch. This is a very important part of selling your ideas. Very few people buy ideas impulsively. Most people need quite some time to consider before making any decision. The norm is to deliberate carefully, or at least look the part. Your job is to cut the "deliberation" process short.

It is important for you to understand that in making decisions, people use intuition, rationality and emotions.

Rationality plays a critical role but not in the expected manner. People do rationalize, by getting information and reflecting on it. However, all this information is eventually set aside and decisions are based on gut feelings.

Once the decision is made, people find explanations for it so they can clarify it to themselves and to others. The decision was based on gut feelings, but the reason "it felt right" is often not good enough. Solid reasons are needed to justify decisions. The subconscious mind is what dictates the need for a good and solid reason. It is this part of the mind that ultimately makes the final decision; whether a "yes" or a "no" is applicable to the idea you are selling. The subconscious needs personal, clear and memorable information before making the decision final. Your job is to influence the subconscious to sway it over to your way of thinking.

To do this, you have to consider how you state your idea. Persuasion is not just about the strength of the idea you are selling. It also depends on how you present it and when. Things that can help include metaphors, sequencing, timing and stories. Make your presentation vivid and easy to remember.

Step 4 – Securing commitments

This is the final step in relationship-based persuasion method. This completes the cycle of the entire method. It takes the situation from agreement to making concrete commitments. This turns your ideas into the desired actions. Your role in persuasion does not end when the other person says "yes". It is just a step towards full realization of your ideas turning into actions. You have to secure commitment. Make sure that the other person follows through with the decision to accept your ideas. Persuasion only becomes successful if the other person adopted your idea and used it to change courses of action and behaviors. Without any action, your persuasion efforts failed.

Chapter 31. Subconscious Techniques in Persuading People

The subconscious has a powerful influence on actions. Learning how to influence this part of a person's mind is a very effective tool in persuasion. You can use this skill in lots of ways- at work, at home, in your social life, making new sales or simply trying to get your friend to join you on a death-defying adventure.

FRAMING

Framing is one of the most basic and commonly used techniques that influence the subconscious. Framing is a technique that alters how people associate, define categorize and sort objects, behaviors or events.

Framing Techniques

Framing can be done in various ways, depending on what you are persuading others about. It also depends on your audience. You can use logic, stories, or for appeal to authorities to convince and persuade people to act in certain ways.

Appeal to logic

Using the power of reasoning is a very effective tool in framing when trying to persuade others. You can use several tools such as assertion, pre-emptive arguments and typecasting.

Assertion

one of the powerful empathic ways to frame a concept, argument or issue. Using words like "the truth is", "the important thing is", "key point is", and "fact is" signal that you are going to say something that is based on facts. This means you should gather information and evidence that supports your arguments. However, not everything that follows these expressions is universally acknowledged as truths. These may be subjective views on the world. For example,

The truth is, we all take life for granted.

> Certainly, it isn't true that everyone takes life of granted. There are people somewhere that know how to appreciate life or just learned to. Most likely, people who are suffering from terminal illnesses or just found they are sick are starting to learn to appreciate life. But, using this statement can prove to be persuasive because people do acknowledge that at times, at some point in their lives, they do take life for granted.

Hence, not everything that follows these words may be a subjective take that may or may not be disputable. You can use purported facts or established information, whatever works in your favor. When you want to be a persuasive speaker, you should know when it is applicable and useful to blur the lines between using subjective statements or established truths.

Pre-emptive arguments

Mean recognizing and acknowledging the opposite side of your argument. It may include bit of sympathizing for the other side and may go as far as identifying with it. Then, use these circumstances to justify why people should take the approach you are advocating. For example:

> I am aware that some people would choose to combat illnesses aggressively with the use of modern technologies and medicines. These have greatly helped a lot of people over the years. These have changed the lives of many. However, this same method of treatment also comes with risks. There are side effects that may

become a more serious problem than the original illness being treated. For example, headache is very effectively and quickly reduced with painkillers. But, long-term use of thee medications can cause bleeding problems and stomach ulcers. This is why it is better to use natural means. These traditional, natural remedies have been used for centuries. These have cured a lot of people too through the years. They are just as effective as modern medicine but with much less risk and side effects.

In the above example, acknowledgement of the other side of the argument, which is modern medicine, is included. Towards the end of the discussion, the speaker used the same opposing side to support the side he is proposing, which is traditional medicine.

Acknowledging counter arguments may also be in the form "not A but B". For example:

- Using makeup is not trying to change who you are, but it is a means of emphasizing the beauty you already have.
- Changing the way we do things around does not mean we weren't being effective. It means we have to adjust to changing needs.
- There is nothing wrong with your favorite brand. But, you may be missing out on other good things by sticking to it.

You get 2 advantages at once when you use this framing technique. One, you appear well reasoned and well informed. It seems you have researched everything well, taking into consideration all sides of the argument. They will consider your proposition as well-informed and well-considered choices, not just simple assertions. The second advantage is that you deal with any possible objections to the solution you are proposing. You have already mentioned the possible arguments for the opposing side and already made explanations for it. This way, you are met with little resistance, saving you from having to go through lengthy discussions.

***Typecasting*, along with *selectivity*, are two powerful framing techniques to use in persuasion.**

Typecasting is more of making generalizations and oversimplifying things. It also entails misleading others and being selective. Despite these, it is a very powerful tool to use in persuasion. It is effective because good vs. bad stories are very compelling, easy to tell and easy to understand. Humans have been primed to see things as 2 opposing forces, where one is good (right) and one is bad (wrong). People don't even have to consider other factors. They just immediately go for the good, right or beneficial side. Typecasting simplifies decision-making. It removes any conflicting and overlapping factors that make decision-making difficult for most.

For example, "Americans love hamburgers" is a form of typecasting. It creates the assumption that each and every American loves hamburgers. It also carries with it a subtle meaning that if you don't like hamburgers, then you are not fully American.

You can use typecasting to the opposing argument. An example is when you are promoting a weight loss method. You keep pushing for the advantages. Talk about the ill effects of excess weight and obesity. Invoke a picture of ugliness, sloppiness and poor productivity in obese people. You are typecasting obese people into slow moving, constantly eating and all-day-TV kind of people. These people are unsuccessful, unhappy and unproductive. Then create an image of happy, successful slim people. They look beautiful, clean and active. By creating the contrast through typecasting, you are moving your audience's mind to be more attracted to the idea that to be happy and successful, they have to be slim. Hence, you will be more successful in persuading them to buy you slimming products.

You can also add selectivity or selective disclosure.
This is where you practice the art of telling only what is likely to be believed. You put more emphasis on portions that support you proposal and downplaying other information. For example, you can cast people who smoke cigarettes in a bad light. You can paint a picture of cigarette smokers looking unkempt with bad hygiene, bad breath, and yellowed teeth. Then, create a more positive image of people who use e-cigarettes. Make them look cool, clean and sophisticated. You talk more about how easy they are to use, and that users can "smoke" everywhere, even in non-smoking areas because it isn't actually smoking. You don't talk about how its safety and long-term effects on health have not yet been fully established. You also downplay the possibility of accidents and risks involved with the use of e-cigarettes. Also, do not mention the fact there is a hot debate on whether using e-cigarettes is the same as smoking or not. Or, that there is a debate on whether to impose the same restrictions on e-cigarettes as those in cigarette smoking. The point is to avoid mentioning stuff that the public is not yet fully aware of (e.g., long-term effects, risks, health, etc.). This is particularly necessary if such information has a negative effect on your persuasion.

Typecasting and selectivity appeal to most people for several reasons. It removes grey areas, intricacies, nuances and subtleties that often complicate things. This method guides others to choosing only between two opposing ideas or concepts. This may not be the ideal, as there are so many details left out. It also entails manipulation, half-truths and omissions. But all the same, a lot of people are drawn to it because it offers simplicity. Another reason is that this method appeals and sways the emotions, which is a potent driving force.

Appeal to authority and Appeal to precedent

This framing method uses reference to authorities and well-known figures. It lends credibility to statements you make. Also, it puts the listener within a more concrete context. It frames the concepts you are presenting, making it more tangible for the listener.

This is a very popular framing method used by motivational speakers, politicians and the like. They quote great men like Gandhi, Martin Luther King and the Dalai Lama. This achieves 2 things at the same time. One, it aligns the speaker with the quoted person. It would seem that the speaker is agreeing with the values and principles that these stand for. For instance, quoting Gandhi gives the impression of aligning with this man's call for peaceful resolution of conflicts. Quoting Steve Jobs gives the impression of aligning with the man's ingenuity and innovativeness.

Two, this framing method lends charisma, authority and wisdom to the speaker's presentation. Citing these well-known figures helps in legitimizing the speaker's own take on things. It also helps to lend credibility to the speaker's claims. It also makes it easier for the public to accept the speaker's statements because these are aligned to already acceptable ideas.

Semantic categories

Mean using different words that have the same general meaning but in varying degrees. It is more commonly known by the expression "depends on what you meant by the word". This is a reflection that even with the same general meaning, different words would come to mean differently and affect others in varying degrees, too. For example, the term "weight loss" and "slim down". At first glance, these terms basically mean the same. However, with semantic categories, "Weight loss" may mean losing weight but not necessarily cause one to become slim. That is, a 3-kilogram weight loss is weight loss. But for someone who is 10 kilograms overweight, this amount of weight loss is not enough to achieve a slim body. Unlike with the term "slim down", it means turning whatever body type into a slim figure

Semantic category is also one of the most widely used framing technique in politics and advertising. It can be through the use of varying terms to mean something. Something more like "saying the same things, only in different ways". People use different terms either to emphasize a point or to tone down it implications. For example, the tern "pro-abortion" carries a negative impression. It makes people who belong to this group seem like they have no regard for human life, and unflinching when it comes to killings. To soften the impact, the term "pro-choice" is now being used. The core values and principles carried by the group remain the same despite the change in name. However, this term gives them a less negative impression to the public.

The Appeal of stories

Stories have long been used in human history. It is not just about entertainment. It is used to explain events, pass down traditions, and tell history. It is also a powerful tool for persuasion.

Why are stories so compelling? They can gain and maintain anyone's attention, especially if framed and timed properly. Defined, a story is fact (or group of facts) that is wrapped in emotions, designed to compel the listeners to act. There are 4 components found in all kinds of stories, each contributing to the power to persuade. There is emotion, found in the manner of telling the story and in the feelings the story evokes in the listener. There is a problem, embodied by a contretemps or antagonist. There is a protagonist, designed to be the one the listeners can identify with. The 4th component is change, which is often the redemption part of the story. Most people are not aware of a 5th component of a story. This is the moment wherein the listeners, as well as the characters, reach awareness. This part is called the epiphany. It is present in the story for just a short time, but is a powerful moment. It is the turning point of the story, where change or redemption starts. All these components are present in any story, including the ones you use to illustrate your point when persuading others.

Persuasion includes stories as a key component. These help in structuring events, builds cohesion and encourage listeners to identify with the actors and the values embodied in the story. It also helps in expanding the horizons through which the speaker and the listeners interact. It evokes identification and cohesiveness through shared experiences and common suffering illustrated in the stories.

Stories used in persuasion are filled with a lot of framing methods. The most common ones used include the use of analogies and metaphors. Images and metaphors trigger emotions, which make them very effective in arousing people to action. It is very advantageous to create a series of images and metaphors. It provides enough information that allows people to infer the rest of the picture. These should serve to guide (manipulate) others into thinking the picture you want them to see.

For example, in a bid to persuade people to believe the ultimate good in the war in Afghanistan, analogies are used.

Afghanistan is being compared to Vietnam, relating the incidents during the Vietnam War as happening again in Afghanistan. Metaphors are also used, in attempts to justify the war and persuade people to believe the justifications. Afghanistan is depicted as a graveyard of nations all over the world. This refers to the fallen soldiers and other personnel belonging to different countries allied together in this war. These are persuasive statements that make people rethink their stand on wars. It evokes memories of Vietnam and how fervently the nation fought. By evoking the image of a graveyard, it acknowledged courage and sacrifice. This example of framing can be very persuasive in changing people's minds, stand and opinions. It is commonly used in politics, especially when trying to present an undesirable policy.

Another technique is the use of implications and connotations. These are less overt methods that can be used to frame arguments well. An example is when discussing taxes. This is a sore subject because this almost always means having to pay more. To reduce tension during discussions and to make the matter more acceptable and less objectionable, terms such as "tax relief" are used. The term "tax relief" suggests the acknowledgement that tax is an affliction. Many people will readily accept this implication because most people feel they are paying too much tax and treat it as a burden. This then implies that anything that can minimize the burden is more of a hero rather than a villain. Nobody can argue well against the implication that tax is a burden or an affliction because every single person has had experience of having to pay more for services and have much less from wages. Any objections only work to solidify and strengthen the framed idea. Just as telling someone not to think of food will only drive a person to think of food, even though he has no intentions or inclinations to do so before you even made the suggestion.

Reframing is even more effective than the abovementioned example. The new frame should be able to appeal to the public's common values. It has been observed that people vote for the side that they can identify with, not for the side that can further their self-interests. Hence, even if people understand that one side is promoting something for the improvement of their lives, they still tend to take the opposing side, if it mirrors their own values. People tend to prefer the side they can call "part of them", or "one of their own". Getting into these closely-knit groups can be pretty difficult. It is equally difficult to get persuade them to your side if they see you as a threat to the values they hold. Hence, in order to persuade people to take your side, you should be able to make them identify with you. This is when you should reframe your arguments so that they can identify with you. When you appeal to values of the "in-group", you are more likely to persuade them.

Connotations

These are similar to metaphors. Connotations are stories contained in a capsule, which bring to mind an entire scenario with just a few sentences. Value judgments are attached to connotations by using carefully chosen words. For example, the terms "civil war" and "rebellion" are short words but attach different value judgments. The meanings are similar but carry different connotations. "Civil war" presents an image of justifiable, rightful unrest with a noble cause for the good of everyone. "Rebellion" evokes an image of a group of rowdy people stirring up trouble for selfish gains. Another example is "terrorist" and "freedom fighter". "Terrorist" calls for images of people out to sow hatred, extort money from governments and individuals, spreads terror and destroys peace. They are depicted as people whose main goal is to spread terror, war and injustice. "Freedom fighters" calls for an image of oppressed people fighting with limited resources but with hearts full of courage to obtain freedom from influential governments that seek to control their society. People who support the war against these groups would refer to them as "terrorists". War against terrorists is justifiable. People who do not support the war efforts would refer to these groups as "freedom fighters". War against freedom fighters is a form of oppression.

Clusivity

This refers to the strategic use of pronouns to suit one's goals. For example, people often use "we" and "us" when trying to diffuse the responsibility over a negative incident or action. Sometimes it is also used to foster identification with the audience. The pronoun "I" is used when trying to get the credit for some exemplary action. The pronoun "them" is often used when trying to establish contrast or drawing the difference from the opposition or competition. The pronoun "you" is often used to challenge or spur the listener to action. This is often done as a closing statement, after manipulating the listeners. Also, this is often only done if the speaker is already confident of successfully persuading or influencing the listeners. A few examples for clusivity are:

- We made the difficult decision of removing you from your position. (diffusing the responsibility of firing the employee)
- I lead the group in the creation of this wonderful ad. (taking a larger chunk of the credit)
- The team and I made all these wonderful benefits possible for the rest of the company. (acknowledging the efforts of others but placed emphasis on the self)
- They tried to take your money through false promises. (making the competitor look bad)

- We should put our health as top priority. (establishing identification with the listeners)
- You decide. (after a riveting speech, already assured that the listeners are convinced)
- You should buy now while supplies last. (spur the listener to action)

Shared aspirations

Aspiration is among the most effective persuasive framing techniques. Most speeches opt to end with this technique, leaving a positive and hopeful feeling on the listeners. This is especially helpful if the entire presentation or speech is filled with serious issues and lots of conflict. It sustains a crescendo, leaving a positive high. People who feel good and hopeful about their future are more receptive to persuasion compared to ones who are depressed. A crescendo is achieved by using heightened language, and filled with numerous alliterations, refrains and the like.

Aspirations are effective because they signal the transition of the argument from the present and into the future. It expands the inclusive circle by projecting insights developed during the presentation into an ideal future.

For example, the presentation is trying to persuade people into investing in a company. The business is about something experimental. People are less likely to make huge investments in businesses that have yet to prove capable of returning investments and earning large profits. You can still make them enthusiastic about an experimental business venture by using aspirations. Capitalize in envisioning a bright future ushered by the business. Another example is persuading people into buying pre-need insurance plans. Most people are hesitant in investing a sizeable amount of money into something they might not even need in the future. Paint a picture wherein they will benefit hugely from the insurance plan. Make them picture a future wherein they will be saved from disappointments, troubles and hassles, all because of the insurance plan they purchase today.

Redress

Redress refers to righting and putting something back on track. This framing technique is often used together with aspiration. It is oriented towards the future. It comes with a powerful core message that everything will turn out all right and an ideal future can be achieved. But, all these can only be achieved if the principles and ideas of the speaker were followed.

Language used in redress framing method is heightened. It is filled with music, imagination and metaphors. It follows the old saying to use poetry when campaigning but use prose when governing. Poetry wins the hearts of the people, persuading them to take your side. It is lyrical and musical, which is pleasant to hear and touches emotions. These are potent combinations in winning and persuading people.

Credibility

This is the final framing, known in Greek as “ethos”. This is the part where the speaker’s credibility will be judged based on the knowledge, evidence presented, credentials and authority. It is a culmination of the entire presentation, which reiterates the points previously discussed. It instills in the mind that everything the speaker has said can be trusted.

REASONS AND EMOTIONS

Appealing to these are also effective tools in persuading others. One most persuasive form is the use of logical fallacies. It is often considered as faulty logic but very effective in persuasion. Propagandas always use this method because it rouses emotions in the listeners.

One example is citing historical and prominent people. It appeals to the emotions and to authority. Listeners are awed by the "rightness" that these people stand for. They are also swayed into thinking about promoting, supporting and emulating these people. Emotions triggered include protective devotion, allegiance and respect, which also rub off to the speaker.

"Iron fist, velvet glove"

This may also apply the Latin concept *fortiter in re, suaviterin modo*, translated as "strong in idea, gracious in method". This is a core concept in effective persuasion, where the persuader cleverly combines grace and force. In order to effectively persuade people, you have to know how and when to use either or both. Force is used when asserting a concept or principle. Grace is applied by practicing attentiveness.

Assertion is done in several ways. It can be asserting what something is through typecasting and labeling. It can be asserting the word meaning or definition. It can be asserting through the interpretation of events and facts through reasoned arguments and logical thinking. These 3 forms of assertion compose the iron fist or force of an argument when persuading others. It is the underlying message. A person who can use all these can effectively maintain control of the issue being discussed.

Grace, in the form of attentiveness, is the velvet glove that covers the iron fist. It is what people immediately see. It is conveyed through the acknowledgement of the other side of the issue, topic or argument. Statements like "as they/you say", "the other party/company/product, etc." and "as you/they/we know" are common ways of acknowledgement. This does not mean you have express agreement. The point is to look as if you are reaching out to your competitor/opponent. It is one way of verbal grooming. This technique does not involve imposing on the opposite side of the topic through demanding or overly direct language. It involves use of subtle reference and indirectness. This helps in maintaining face, in case things prove otherwise in the near future. It also gives freedom to maneuver, especially when faced with aggressive or persistent objections.

Assertion is used when giving force or firmness to the topic. It is backed by evidence. Attentiveness is expressed through the use of inclusive benefits and shared aspirations.

It is a method of describing or explaining things in specific ways in order to influence how others interpret information. It involves using certain words in order to alter perception on what the speaker is saying.

Framing consists of 3 fundamental elements- placement, approach and method.

> *Placement* refers to choosing the right place, people and time in order to maximize the effectiveness of framing techniques.
>
> *Approach* refers to the presentation method used. Generally, people respond better when statements, topics or issues are presented in a positive manner compared to those presented negatively.
>
> *Method* refers to the use of specific words to increase the effectiveness of persuasion. Some words tend to be more persuasive. The manner these words are spoken in also influences the success or failure of persuasion. When people hear words, the brain can separate the

words and the intonation used on these words. The brain then processes the information separately.

TIMING

When you talk to people is as important as *what* you tell them about. People tend to be more agreeable, submissive and easy to persuade when they are already mentally tired. Wait until someone has just finished something mentally taxing before asking him or her for something or trying to persuade them. For example, catch a colleague as they are walking out the door after a long day at work. They are likely to respond that they'll take care of it tomorrow. When trying to persuade people to buy certain products in groceries, choose those that look exhausted. Chances are, they'd just buy whatever it is you are offering just so they can move on. They do not have the energy to listen to long presentations and discussions. So, they'll likely just agree. Their minds can no longer formulate any good objection, so you'll likely deal with less resistance.

CONGRUENCE

Congruence is acting in ways consistent with one's previous actions. To illustrate, notice that most salespeople shake their potential client's hands even before they start their sales pitch. Handshakes in negotiations often signify that a deal has been closed. Hence, the handshake before negotiations even began is signaling the subconscious that a deal has already been made. This is setting the mind up for an agreeable outcome. The potential buyer is then conditioned to agree in the end, even before hearing out what the salesperson has to say.

Another example is letting the client hold the item. This is pretty much as if he already took the item from the shelf to buy it. This action simulates the usual series of actions involved when actually buying things. That is, taking the item, holding it and then eventually paying for it. This way, you are more likely to persuade the person to buy the product.

FLUID SPEECH

Fluid speech is talking with minimal interjections. This means limiting the "uummms" and "uuhhs". It also means keeping he "like" and "I mean" to bare minimum. These little words and interjections are often unnoticed but have a strong effect on the subconscious. The unintended effect is that you will seem unsure of yourself and do not have full confidence in what you are saying. You will less successful in your attempt at persuasion. People are more likely to be persuaded by a speaker who is confident in what he says.

HERD BEHAVIOR

Herd behavior refers to the tendency to perform actions or think in certain ways because everybody else does. This stems from the inherent need to belong, identify with others and to be accepted. Humans are social beings. Hence, they make attempts to blend in or be part of a group. This need drives herd behavior. Also, it is more possible for people to be persuaded by someone they like or see as an authority figure.

You can use herd behavior by appearing as the group's leader. You don't have to have the official title. All you have to do is to act like one. Initiate the behavior you want others to exhibit. For example, you want to persuade your staff to work harder and change the way things go in the office. Instead of making speeches, take the lead and exhibit the changes you want others to do.

It also helps to be confident and charming. People are more attracted to a person who exudes appositive vibe. The pleasure they get from being around you is a powerful tool in persuasion. They will also treat your opinions and views with greater weight and respect.

POWER OF DRINKS

Offer drinks (if the situation is conducive for drinks) to the person you want to persuade. Ever wondered why people often offer drinks when they talk to someone, using the classic line "Do you want something to drink? Coffee, tea or juice?" Drinks play a role in persuasion, too.

Warm drinks in a cold environment provide a warm and comforting sensation. This will subconsciously associate the warmth with you. They will see you as a warm, welcoming and likeable person. This will make them feel comfortable around you. They'd likely pay attention to what you say and readily agree to you. Cool, refreshing drinks on a hot day will evoke refreshing, cool feelings in the person you are trying to persuade. They'd see your ideas as new and refreshing, too. Your ideas, even if experimental, unorthodox or totally radical, will receive better reception.

Giving cold drinks on cold days or warm drinks on warm drinks has the opposite effect. It will increase their discomfort. They will likely feel uncomfortable in your presence, making them less agreeable to what you are telling them. They'd be too distracted to pay much attention to you, too.

ASKING THE RIGHT QUESTIONS

Start a conversation on a positive note. Ask questions that will generate a "Yes". Examples include:

- "Nice weather today, isn't it?"
- "You want to be healthier, don't you?"

- "You are looking for great deals on cars, aren't you?"
- "You have a great kid there, don't you?"

The "yes" at the beginning of a conversation sets its tone. It also creates a positive momentum. A "Yes" at the start is likely to continue until the final "Yes, I'll buy that one" or "Yes, I'm in".

THE TOUCH BARRIER

Touch plays an important role in persuasion. It can strengthen connections you built or break the deal. Appropriate touches at the right time will help seal the deal. It should be subtle and within social and personal boundaries. The safest and most widely used touch is the handshake. It is personal, yet business-like, firm but amiable. Touch, in the right context and at the right time, fulfills the natural human need to bond.

Sometimes, touch might be seen as a form of harassment or invasion of personal space. Study the person carefully to see if the person is the touching kind. You can see this the moment you approach. If you see the other person back away a little or flinch when you move towards his/her direction, then it is a likely indication they do not want to be touched or get too close. Also, notice if they cross their arms over their chest. This is a defensive mode, closing themselves to your attempts at persuasion and influence. This is also a good indication that they do not welcome physical touch.

In instances when you don't know if physical touch will be welcomed or not, you can still touch in a different level. You can use praises and compliments as a means of verbal touching,

These subconscious techniques have been proven by lots of people. These are effective ways in easily persuading people to think or act in certain ways. When used in the right context, to the right people at the right time, you can practically control others easily and with minimal effort.

Chapter 32. The Art of Negotiating

Negotiating is another skill that can help you to persuade people. This isn't exactly giving in to what the other person wants. In fact, most people use negotiation as a form of persuasion. It can be used to get more out of something than was initially available. For example, a person may not be convinced enough to buy something from you. With the right negotiation skills, you can get the other person to buy what you have initially offered and something else, too.

To start off with, negotiation is a process of settling differences. Compromise or agreements are reached to avoid disputes and arguments. It is natural for people to want to get the best advantage or outcome possible in any disagreement. Each person in a disagreement will want to get the most out of the situation. By entering into a negotiation, each party walks away with the best possible benefits.

By changing the way you see negotiation. you will be able to hone your skills and achieve better and more satisfying results. Negotiation is not always about making a series of compromises that ends in someone winning and someone losing. By offering win-win solutions, you get to be more effective in persuading people. By turning negotiations into a joint problem solving activity, people will be more open to your suggestions, more trusting and more receptive to your ideas. If you take a battlefield stance in negotiations, the other party would likely be in the defensive mode, actively trying to oppose your ideas and will likely be very resistant, thinking that you are manipulating them in order to get your own selfish ends.

Outcomes are more consistent and satisfactory, too. You form good interpersonal relationships. People feel good doing business with you and soon, more people will be attracted to you and be more receptive of your ideas.

You can achieve all these if you learn to recognize different behavioral, negotiation and communication styles. This way, you get to adjust your own approach to match the other person's style.

TIPS TO SUCCESSFUL NEGOTIATION

These tips can help you be a successful negotiator, with most of the benefits from an agreement working for you.

#1 Negotiating is not all about making compromises
The "zero sum process" is the most commonly used method in negotiation. In this process, you determine what you want and then raise it by 10 or 15% before entering a negotiation. Tough negotiators who negotiate to win use this method. The goal is not to reach a mutually beneficial compromise. The ultimate goal is winning.

The negotiator puts most of the effort into maintaining the position, claiming as much of the situation as possible. This can be a very stressful stance but for people who get what they what, this is highly effective. The point is to get the most advantage and be in the lead position in the negotiation. Asking what one wants and why is not taken into consideration. There isn't even consideration of why the other person is negotiating and what he stands to gain. It is all about getting what you want.

Skilled negotiating is defined as communicating back and forth, sharing some interests and opposing others. Interest in a negotiation is **why** something should happen and not **what** should happen. Most people do not understand this concept. Negotiating is not about WHAT should be achieved.

It is all about the WHY. Once interests are established, negotiation can proceed on working out solutions and looking for alternatives in order to achieve the WHY.

Some people think that each party telling their WHY's is synonymous to laying all the cards on the table and then arguing over who gets the most.

#2 People skills make a huge difference
Negotiating works best if you have good people skills. You have to have a good understanding of how your own actions and behavior can affect others. This can help you in strategizing and adjusting your negotiation in order to be successful.

It is equally important to understand and accept that each person has his own preferred communication method that is uniquely his own. No two persons communicate in exactly the same manner. There are differences, subtle or obvious. This means that you can't always choose the communication method you want. You will have to deal with people who communicate in a different way that may not be to your liking. By understanding and accepting this fact, you will be able to adjust to these differences and still be able to control the situation. This is one of the greatest characteristics that make a highly effective, successful skilled negotiator. These people can quickly adjust their communication methods in order to meet the needs of their listeners and eventually win them over.

Behavior and interaction methods can be classified into 4 categories. These are dominant, influence, steadiness and conscientious.

> ***Dominant*** people are those who have excellent decision-making skills. They are driven by the desire to take control of their environment. They use their

problem-solving skills and take on challenges as a way of gaining control.

People who are dominant interact with others in a direct manner. Telling others what to do is also a part of their communication strategy. They have a lot of confidence in themselves, which often comes off as arrogance or intimidation. These people do not often listen or question when dealing with other people.

Dominants achieve goals in a single direction. They do not often stop to consider multiple outcomes or solutions. They stick to what they think should be done and go for it, often taking the most direct route without any regard to other factors. Their approach is focused on the bottom line, which is the achievement of a goal. They are quick to point out reasons why an approach or method will not work. This characteristic makes others see them as uncaring, ruthless and impatient. They are often considered as negative people. All these are of no huge concern to dominants. What matters to them is getting results rather than considering how others would feel.

Influencers are people who are good at telling but not as direct as dominants. They interact with people through convincing and motivating. They are less likely to coerce people into doing something. Their main focus is on working with people to achieve a goal or complete specific tasks, rather than on getting results.

People categorized as influencers are best described as visionaries. These people see possibilities when a concept or plan is presented to them. They see what can be done rather than what can go wrong.

Influencers and dominants are both considered as leaders but often considered as being on opposite sides of the spectrum. Both have good decision and problem-solving skills but achieve goals in different ways. Influencers see dominants as negative people, while dominants see influencers as "political" or "unrealistic." Influencers lead through developing good relationships with others, focusing on making encouraging, positive impressions on the people they deal with. They want to establish relationships. However, they often seem disorganized and impulsive. They often do not give much attention to details because they prefer to see the bigger picture. They do not dwell on the nitty gritty of things.

Influencers are considered social people. That is, they like to interact with people and tend to have a wide network of friends, contacts and acquaintances. They are also result-oriented but they are more concerned about motivating others to get these results.

Steadiness relates to people similar to influencers. They look at the positive aspects of new ideas, plans or concepts. However, people who deal in steadiness are reluctant to accept changes, even if the change is a positive one. While influencers are leaders, steadiness people are less inclined to lead. They feel they are not powerful enough to make people act. They feel they are less powerful than the environment they are in. They have the idea that everything will go well only if people work harder together following a status quo.

Steadiness people are excellent at listening to what others have to say. Before they respond, steadiness people stop and ruminate on things, taking into consideration all possible angles. They take their time before responding or making any decision. Dominant and influencers would have to deal with steadiness people more cautiously. They do not want to be rushed. They are reserved and very methodical.

They are also people-focused, like influencers are. Steadiness people are very dependable and are very solid team players. They work well with others.

Conscientious people are similar to steadiness people. They are reserved people and very introverted. They also share a similarity with dominants. They are focused on control and getting tasks done. These people are considered perfectionists. They want things done and their approach is reserved, diplomatic, business-like and indirect.

Negotiating with conscientious people is best done by giving facts and sticking to specific points. They do not readily accept anything. It is pretty difficult to change their minds, especially if reasoning is weak and not supported by figures and facts.

Conscientious people operate on the idea that problems are easily solved and change is not necessary if only people will stick to procedures and processes. They are tough sticklers to rules and SOPs. For them, processes and facts that support points and steps are most important. People and establishing relationships are secondary considerations.

Understanding these categories can greatly help in negotiating successfully. For instance, an influencer who is negotiating with a conscientious person would have to be armed with facts and figures to support points, information and claims. This may prove difficult for influencers, as they are not strong when it comes to details. Dominants would have more success when negotiating with conscientious people. The attention to detail, drive to arrive at a decision and the persistence to achieve results are keys to successful negotiations between dominants and conscientious people. A limiting factor, however, with conscientious people is that their need for facts may make them appear indecisive.

People who have different styles are likely to find it difficult in interacting well. For example, an influencer dealing with a conscientious person may produce negative results. He may make some remarks about a minor statistic regarding product qualities. This remark is likely to be challenged by the conscientious person. The influencer, being less adept at details, may not be able to defend the remark. The conscientious person, seeing that the remark is weak because of lack of supporting facts, would likely be uninterested and walk away. A steadiness person who is negotiating with a dominant may not achieve his goals. The dominant person tends to keep talking, moving forward with a plan or concept. The steadiness would need time to ponder on the information and answers to any questions. The dominant person is miles away from the point the steadiness is still pondering on because of his natural tendency to fill the silence and proceed head-on towards achievement of a goal or arriving at a decision. An influencer dealing with a dominant may also find it difficult to hold the dominant's attention. Influencers tend to answer questions with anecdotes, long-winded stories or indirect examples. Dominants prefer a direct approach. To be a skilled negotiator, you have to learn to recognize to what category you belong to and to what category the other person belongs to. Adjust accordingly. Also, there is the Classic Profile that you can use in order to ramp up your negotiating skills.

The Classic Profile

Experts at negotiation hold a belief that people possess all of the characteristics of the abovementioned categories. The difference among these is which attribute/s is more intense. For example, a dominant person also tends to crave for facts like conscientious people do, with methodical like steadiness and can see the bigger picture like influencers do. However, their most intense attribute is result-oriented, which categorizes them as dominant. This is called the Classic Profile.

This profile gives a complete picture to the negotiator, in which to base strategies. It provides an idea of behavioral tendencies and what communication styles would work best. The Classic Profile provides an evaluation of a person's style and behavior within the context of the following:

- Goals
- Emotions
- Fears
- Influencing others
- Judging others
- Tendencies that can be overused
- Value to an organization
- Behavior under pressure
- How to increase effectiveness

One or more of these attributes can be used. Learning what to use and when to use them is very crucial when developing successful negotiating skills.

#3 Listening is indispensable

This skill is the single most powerful skill to develop when trying to influence, manipulate, control, motivate, negotiate with or persuade others. This is a great tool to learn about the other person's interests. It can also help you to gauge what type of person you are dealing with, what his communication methods are and how best to approach the person.

Most people fail to see the importance of good listening skills when dealing with people. They barge ahead with their sales pitch, long list of facts and figures and other strategies to win people over. They forget to listen. And when they do, they only listen so that they can reply but not listen to understand what the person is trying to tell them.

A study in UCLA led by Dr. Albert Mehrabian illustrated the mismatch in how people ordinarily communicate. When people communicate, ideas and feelings are conveyed in several ways- through words, the tone of the voice and body language. This study showed the following breakdown:

- Words: 7%
- Tone of Voice: 38%
- Body Language: 55%

This means that only 7% of the message is conveyed through words. A huge majority, 93% of meanings and messages are conveyed through non-verbal means (i.e., tone of the voice and body language). For most, they focus more on verbal communication, missing out on the huge chunk of the message conveyed through non-verbal means. Listening does not only mean hearing the spoken words but also studying, understanding and interpreting the non-verbal cues as well.

Listening skills

There are 3 levels of listening you can use in order to understand what the other person is trying to tell you. You can also use these in order to obtain more information.

Listening can help you learn about the interests of the other person. This is helpful while you are enhancing your negotiation skills. One great way in practicing your listening skills is asking questions. Ask questions and listen closely to both verbal and non-verbal messages. Asking questions is crucial to get more information and learn more about other people. For effective questioning, 3 factors should occur:

- Good understanding of the direction the questions will take. Random questions often unnerve a lot of people. Instead of getting and holding their attention, random questions will only cause confusion and consequently increase discomfort. It can make you look like you are unsure, trying to bait people or fishing around hoping for something of value to come up. Instead of engaging other people, it makes people distrust you.
- Ask if it is okay to ask questions. Going up to people and firing question after question can unnerve, surprise or confuse people. Before you start questioning someone, ask politely if they mind answering a few questions. Get their consent first. This way, they will be more prepared and more cooperative.
- Inform people what kind of information you want to know. Before asking questions, give a person an overview, a general idea of what you want to obtain from them. For example, tell a person that you just want to find out their preferences when they shop for food. This way, you are establishing the direction of the questioning, putting them at ease. It also helps in gaining their trust.

Once you have established a good environment for asking questions, learn to listen. Remember that most of the message is conveyed through non-verbal means. Also, recognize that listening happens in 3 levels. Use these levels in order to obtain different types of information you use to adjust your strategies, learn more about the other person and eventually know what method to use in order to win them over.

Selective listening is hearing only those you want to hear. This is listening and retaining information that you deem important and relevant to your purpose.

Responsive listening is listening while showing signs that you are indeed listening. You provide physical and verbal feedback to the person you are talking to. Nodding, saying "Tell me more about that" and other leading statements, prompting and making encouraging comments are some ways of showing you are listening and are interested.

Playback means restating what the person said, in your own words, according to how you understood the statement. This is a way to confirm that you have understood what the other person was saying. It is also very helpful if you give a follow up question to confirm, such as "Did I get everything right or did I miss something?" You can use this style as a mini-close to your conversation or line of questioning. This can also work in your favor if an issue arises later into the negotiation. You can say, "I missed that" or "We talked about that earlier and agreed on this. Is there something we missed or you want to more about?" This can greatly help you in managing any hesitations or doubts that may come in the way of persuading others.

Questioning and listening skills greatly help in negotiations and in ultimately persuading others. These helps in making others talk, which helps to get information that you can use to formulate your strategy to persuade. You can effectively and easily persuade others if you have enough information about others. Also, you can use these skills to make others trust you. It keeps the tension low, allowing the other person to be more receptive to your persuasion and manipulation. They are likely to engage in business with you because they will see you as trustworthy and an effective problem-solver. They feel that you can help them solve their problems and get what they want.

#4 Plan before negotiating.

Very few people develop a plan before they enter into negotiations. Sellers need to develop a plan before they start marketing their products and approaching potential buyers. Persuasion is more successful if careful strategizing is done beforehand.

Planning in this context does not mean determining costs, length of time involved or number of walk-aways. This step means making a detailed plan that attempts to determine what target people may want, why and how you can persuade them to choose to do business with you.

A successful negotiating plan should include the following:

Negotiating style that suits the profile of the target party

Think of the general profile of your target and what communication style will work best. That is, establish if your target is a dominant or an influencer, a steadiness or conscientious person. This will greatly help in planning the best communication style to use. If there isn't enough information to profile the other party, then make an educated guess. This might prompt you to make several plans so you can be prepared for any situation. You will have to make adjustments as you go along.

Think of your interests

This refers to why you want something to happen. Study all your interests and see which ones you should push first and how.

Think of the possible interests of the target person

This is one of the major parts in planning for negotiations. Think of what the interests of the party might be. This helps in determining what interests can be shared and what should be opposed. The opposing interests are the ones that would be negotiated. Focus your attention and efforts on these, not on interests that both parties already share.

Think of interests you can trade

Negotiating would require you to give in to some of the interests of the other party in order to gain something more valuable. Before you enter into negotiations, determine which of your interests have lesser value that may be of higher value to the other party. This way, you are prepared ahead of time about what you can easily trade without suffering or losing any of your more valuable interests. You may even use this as leverage- offering something of higher value to the other party that is of lesser value to you. Simply put, think of something you can give away that will not hurt your interest but is very desirable to the other person. For example, you can easily give small inexpensive trinkets in exchange to persuading someone to buying something more expensive. The trinket may be small and does not cost much, but the gesture is considered as valuable for the other person.

Give and take is part of negotiating. By preparing, you will have a less stressful time and you also get to ensure that you will not be compromising something crucial to your ultimate goal. Decisions are easier and made more quickly because you already have an idea of what can be compromised and what should not be.

People who do not take this step often have poor negotiation skills. They are often those who tend to get less from the bargain. These people also tend to want to go through positional compromises in an attempt to retain interests that are of higher value to them.

Establishing BATNA (Best Alternative to a Negotiated Agreement)

This is crucial to negotiation. BATNA or Best Alternative to a Negotiated Agreement is your alternative position or action you plan to take in case the negotiation fails or an agreement is not reached.

Whatever you accept in the negotiation should always be better than your BATANA. Otherwise, why should you go on negotiating? Accepting something less than your BATNA means you have agreed to something worse than you could have done all by yourself. It is a 100% loss on your part if you do this.

Also, consider what the other party's BATNA might be. Think it through and use it to your advantage. Why are they negotiating with you? Why can't they do it on their own, or why aren't they just walking away? Think of what they can possibly gain by doing business with you and capitalize on it. For example, you are negotiating on prices. Why is it that they are spending time negotiating the price with you and why can't they just walk away and buy elsewhere at an established price? Maybe they are in need of the product.

Capitalize on why they might want the product. Highlight the advantages they can get from it in order to justify the price you are asking.

#5 Know the 10 Factors for effective negotiation.

To be a successful at negotiations, you should:

- Establish your goals and interests. – You should be able to determine what you want to accomplish before you go into a negotiation. Knowing where you are going helps in guiding you towards success.
- Learn about the other side. – Find out what you can about the other person. Learn about how they negotiate, the skills they have, aspirations, fears, hopes, interests and backgrounds. This is valuable information that can help you determine what tactics you can use to get them to agree. These may be little things but can mean winning or losing in the negotiation.
- Timing and method of negotiation – Timing is everything. This holds so true when negotiating. This helps in alerting the game, turning it into a win-win situation. Make it a problem-solving condition by using interests rather than positions. This way you can get the best outcome with the full cooperation of the other party.
- Point-by-point preparation – Nothing beats a carefully planned negotiation strategy. People who plan ahead before heading into a negotiation outperform those who don't. In fact, half the battle is actually fought before you even meet the other party. Go through every possible scenario and strategize on how handle these so that when it does happen during the negotiation, you have a well-prepared action to address the issue.

- Offer the other party benefits for accepting your offers. – Providing benefits for the other party if they accept what you offer is a huge leap towards successful negotiation. You are highly likely to close a negotiation deal if you give them the "what's in it for them." These are more perks that they get immediately after they agree or as a long term benefit if they choose to agree to your terms.
- Frame negotiations around 1-2 key points – Your interests in the negotiation should focus on 1-2 key points. This limits the points that you and the other party would have to discuss. Too many points can easily derail the negotiation. It will just confuse both of you. And the longer you spend negotiating on several points, the more likely you are to lose track of why you are negotiating in the first place. Issues and sub-issues can easily creep up when you are arguing over a long list of points. Keep things simple.
- Establishing your BATNA – Your BATNA is your fallback when negotiations fail. This will be your defining moment that will tell you when it is time to walk away. People with effective negotiating skills know when to walk away and still leave the relationship intact.
- Preparing options for mutual gains – The most successful negotiation is when both parties win. Think of ways as to how both you and the other party gain something from the negotiation. Work around any oppositions or hindrances so that both your interests meet.
- Listen – This is the most powerful skill that you can use in any negotiation. This helps in learning about the

other party's interest, what interests oppose yours, and what can be done for the interests to meet.

Guidelines to Ethical Negotiation

Some people are hesitant to enter negotiations and push for their interests. They feel that they might be harming others if they follow their own interests. For example, you have 2 clients. They want the same thing but in varying degrees. Say, they want to lease the store space. You have 2 spaces available, one bigger and the other is much smaller. Client 1 is a small business about to start a storefront. He can only afford to pay for the smaller store space. Client 2 is a much larger business looking to expand. He wants to rent the larger space as a reception area and the smaller space as a backroom office. Client 1 has to wait for his bank loan to be approved before he can make payments for the store space. Client 2 has the money ready, enough to cover 2 years of rent and he wants both store spaces or will rent none at all. How would you negotiate in this situation? Your own interest is to get both store spaces rented in the soonest possible time. If you give in to Client 1, you would have to find another client to rent the bigger space. This can take time and much effort on your part. If you go with Client 2, you have both spaces rented at once but you risk losing a good relationship with Client 1 who sees you as his only opportunity to get his interest addressed (i.e., having a storefront for his business).

Negotiation, as has been previously explained, is more about jointly solving problems so each party wins. To do this, sometimes, ethical issues may arise, as in the above example. The best possible scenario for this is to find ways to negotiate with Client 2 while securing a good relationship with Client 1. Here is where determining the WHYs of each party comes into consideration. The "WHYs" are the interests of each party, or the reason for entering into a negotiation. The

"What" is not the most important issue in a negotiation. It is about what motivates a person to want to enter the negotiation. And relationships are more important than just getting profits.

Are relationships important considerations when negotiating? The answer is yes. Whether you are seeking long-term business or a one-time transaction, leaving a good impression and forming good relationships can help. You get more clients who want to do more business with you. Satisfied clients can put in a good word about you to other potential clients or to your superiors. Caring for clients is part of good business practice, both to attract new clients and to keep old clients returning. It isn't a good thing to profit from people and then turn your back on them.

However, there are instances when you might be forced to forego relationships. It may be a life and death situation if survival is on the line or when the business is hanging in the balance. In these instances, how should you act? What line do you follow when you are in a desperate position? Most people would put their own interests first in an instant, forgetting about morals and ethics.

Are you supposed to follow ethics and morals and go against your own interests? It isn't necessary to do so. You can still promote your own interests while remaining within ethical practices and retaining morality in your negotiations. How? It all depends on the attitude. You can still work within ethical and moral standards and still promote your interests. What you do does not matter a lot, what matters is how you do things, which depends on your behavior. For example, you have to drop your long-term client in favor of someone else for higher profits because you needed the money to keep your business afloat. At first glance, this may seem unethical because long-term clients are often prioritized. Dropping old clients for bigger profits may seem a bad business move. But, you can still remain ethical in this situation. It depends on how you do it.

According to the Red and Blue Theory, people behave in 4 basic ways. Each category has positive and negative attributes.

SOFTER RED BEHAVIORS

Positive Attributes

- Has interest in others
- Good listener
- Helpful, constructive and cooperative
- Open, informative and approachable
- Patient
- Able to see the positive side in other people

Negative Attributes

- Gives too much concern to other people
- Tends to lose sight of own interest
- Allow others to set agendas
- Naïve, too trusting
- Tends to blame himself
- Self-deprecating
- Easily gives up and becomes disillusioned

AGGRESSIVE RED BEHAVIOR

Positive Attributes

- Determined to obtain the best for one's self
- Audacious and decisive
- Likes to take charge
- Has presence
- Likes to face good challenges
- Has enough stamina and able to deal with stress well
- Performs well during a crisis

Negative Attributes

- Tramples others in pursuit of own interests
- Ignores ideas and interests of the other party
- May bully, coerce or threaten others in the pursuit of interest
- Stressed, intransigent and inflexible
- Manipulative, impulsive and impatient

DEVIOUS RED BEHAVIOR

Positive Attributes

- Has the ability to respond quickly to opportunities
- Analytical
- Seeks to educate other people to be prudent
- Avoids publicly humiliating the other party
- Plays and negotiates well using a game plan
- Looks only after own interest

Negative Attributes

- Self-seeking and often resorts to cheating

- Disregards interests, concerns and ideas of others
- Likes to plot and manipulate
- Creates suspicion and cynicism
- Tends to exploit people who are careless and innocent
- Clever
- Ethically confused

ASSERTIVE BLUE

Positive Attributes

- Has good skills in probing and questioning
- Imaginative
- Flexible and adaptable
- Persuasive
- Has the ability to see new options and opportunities
- Wants to make things work
- Does not easily surrender
- Adept at "thinking on his feet"
- Seeks to get the deal
- Good at making creative trade-offs
- Able to lower confrontations by switching between issues

Negative Attributes

- Lacking in firmness
- May come off as phony

- May sometimes be offensive
- Compromising
- Too pushy and too charming
- Tends to adopt a lot of ideas, often unsound, and abandons them quickly
- Too imaginative
- May seem lacking in substance and commitment
- Often seeks to link one issue to another instead of standing firm long enough to find a resolution

While these behaviors are clearly defined, in reality, no one behaves in a single manner all the time. A person may be dominant, with mostly aggressive red behaviors. However, at times, this same person may exhibit other behaviors, depending on the situation.

Generally, a person is motivated to exhibit red behaviors when:

- The other person exhibits blue behavior and there is a desire to exploit
- The other person exhibits red behavior and there is a desire to protect himself, often in the form of a counterattack

Generally, a person exhibits blue behavior when:

- The other person exhibits blue behavior and there is a desire to cooperate
- The other person exhibits behaviors difficult to classify. Risk is taken by exhibiting blue behavior in order to foster cooperation (some opt to risk by exhibiting red behavior if the other person's style is undetermined)

These motivations are fueled by feelings, driving a person to exhibit any of these behaviors. These feeling become so intense that often people no longer think about what is moral or ethical. When people become frightened, happy, anxious, or scared, nothing else becomes more important. In fact, interests are driven by feelings.

For red behaviors:

A person motivated to act in red style because of the desire to exploit someone exhibiting blue behaviors is fueled by feelings of greed.

A person motivated to exhibit red behaviors to protect himself because the other person is exhibiting red behaviors is fueled by feelings of fear.

For blue behavior:

Exhibiting blue behaviors to foster cooperation is fueled by feelings of trust.

Risking by exhibiting blue behaviors implies feeling courageous.

In general, red behaviors are driven by negative feelings and blue behaviors are fueled by positive feelings. Hence, it is difficult to be moral and ethical when there are negative feelings. When negotiations and interests depend on feelings, it is hard to consider ethics and morality. Thus, a person will have to consider 2 things:

- What are the interests and how powerful are these?
- What are the feelings regarding these interests and the situation?

It is difficult to alter the interests because it involves a lot of factors that go beyond the current situation. It is based on past experiences, influenced by present circumstances and driven by hopes for the future. Altering them would mean manipulating several factors at once. What one can do is to control the feelings behind these interests. Controlling the feelings can control attitudes and behaviors behind the interests. Thinking if behaviors are good or bad may be difficult because sometimes what is good for the self may be bad for others. But when feelings are controlled, ethics and morality will come naturally.

The Ethics of Negotiating

Ethics is very important in doing business, even in today's aggressive business world. High standards should be applied to thoughts, negotiation styles and behaviors. Compromised values in business are all too common nowadays. Lots of companies boast huge profits and minimal losses because they do business without considering morality and ethics. Aggressive and uncaring business practices may earn huge profits but it will not sustain the business. Ethical business dealings may not earn huge profits early into the business but it will sustain the business and will eventually help in huge profits later.

To maintain high standards when dealing with others, consider these 4 basic ideas:

The Common Good

The Common Good refers to situations where the effect on other people of one's actions is taken into consideration. Good for others (e.g., clients, staff, customers, employees, etc.) is prioritized over the company's own desires and needs.

In reality, egos get in the way of thinking and acting for the common good. One's ego overshadows the desire to build good relationships and follow good business practices. It gets in the way of providing quality service and treating others fairly. Some people use their egos to manipulate and persuade others to do things that are unethical.

Before you do business, manipulate and persuade others, stop and ask yourself why. Are you doing this for yourself, for your own gains or because you want to make a difference? Are you manipulating others so you can earn huge profits for your own needs and desires or are you doing this because you want to help others achieve their own goals, too? For example, you persuade others to buy your products so that you will get rich or you persuade others to patronize your products so you can keep the business running and provide jobs to more people?

Egos can get in the way when considering all these things. When you no longer serve the common good, when all you want is to achieve your personal goals without any regard to the effects of your actions on others, you may be sacrificing long-term loss for short-term gain. Unethical, selfish practices give you and your business a bad reputation. Word gets around and soon people will avoid doing business with you. Think: Your immediate profit is not enough to cover for a damaged reputation. Your business will eventually fail and people forget about the products and services you once offered. But people will always remember your reputation for ruthless, uncaring business practices.

Therefore, it is very crucial to consider others. It helps to maintain ethical balance when dealing with others. Ask, “What can be done to get others to cooperate?” How much you give determines how much you get. You can never go astray when you put other people’s feelings and welfare first before your own. Yes, it is inevitable you lose some or a lot in the pursuit of the common good, but the long-term gains will fully compensate for all the losses.

Communal Wisdom

Communal wisdom involves looking at the bigger picture. People often fail to see it because they are so focused on immediate concerns and short-term goals. They think narrowly when they make decisions. They think that the only way or the best approach is their own approach or method. When they do ask for suggestions, they get them from people they know are in favor of their practices. That is, they obtain suggestions and ideas from people they know think a lot like them or always agree with them.

It is important to surround oneself with people whose only desire is to do what is right. You should include people who are concerned for your wellbeing and not just people who agree to you. Advice from people who want to do the right things for you is invaluable. It helps to keep you on the right path and prevents you from missing out on what is most important.

Be open to their honesty, genuine concern and perspectives. This is unselfish advice that can help you, especially when you are facing ethical dilemmas, issues, situations or questions. Tapping into their wisdom can often easily solve these problems.

Tapping into communal wisdom can also help you cut through the learning curve. This way, you get to move forward faster with your goals, and find it easier and will experience fewer bumps along the road. You can even save yourself from a lot of pain, disappointments and failures.

Be True to yourself

Staying true to yourself, what you are and what you value helps in being ethical and moral throughout your dealings. A person is the sum total of all experiences and influences throughout their life. People you have been with, met or talked to, as well as the relationships you have formed through the years and all the experiences you've been through influence your value system. All these factors are also considered when you make decisions. All these things instill attitudes, perceptions, insights and values. These influences also help shape you as an individual, which also includes how you deal and do business with others. These play important roles in how you build and conduct your business.

Positive experiences help in building positive values. You should stay true to these values and perceptions. However, life is not always about positive things. Negative experiences are also part of life. The challenge with negative experiences is making a choice. You have to choose if you want to continue the path where negativities take you or to learn from these and use these to become better. Also, a negative situation can be an opportunity to examine oneself and have an attitude check. Take it as a chance to examine yourself and see what areas need to be improved and what areas to remove.

Whatever the circumstances, always stay true to your core values. It may mean giving up some opportunities or losing some profits but it will give you a better sense of accomplishment. You may lose a little but your values are your ticket to greater gains in the future.

Your values do not mean these are absolutely right and should be followed in each and every situation. These are your guidelines, your fall back when confusion arises or when you are faced with negative choices. They are meant to help you keep focus on what you should do - a lifeline to keeping your dealings within ethical and moral standards. Take a look at the Constitution. It has sets of laws meant to guide and create an orderly society. How the laws are applied is, however, variable. It can also be amended to suit the changing needs of society, taking into consideration the changes and progress of society. The same is true with your values. It is the essence of who you are and what you hold dear, but it has to be flexible. For example, you value honesty. But there is a difference between being honest and being tactless. There is also the timing and the situation where you should be honest. For example, honesty in providing product specifications is good. But telling the negative aspects of the competitor's products, however true, may be seen as bad business practice. It may come off as trying to destroy the competitor to make your own product look better. Honesty when trying to persuade people to buy your products or avail of the services you offer is commendable. However, honesty in pointing out the flaws of target customers just to make a point is very much unwelcome. For example, you are trying to persuade people to buy a skin care product. Honesty in telling that effectiveness and results vary among individuals is admirable. Some skin types may respond better to the product and some may not show any improvements at all. However, telling one's target client that your product will not be effective for him because his skin has serious issues may come off as insulting and hurtful. Hence, you need to weigh the circumstances if you can apply your values and adjust accordingly. Sometimes, situations may prompt you to re-evaluate your values, and may also prompt you to take a new direction. For example, honesty is the value you hold most when dealing with people. Are you going to be absolutely honest when you know it will hurt someone? For example, you know that the competitor is doing all it can, even cutting corners, just to get the same client you want. This competitor is desperate because his entire business is on the line. He needs to close a deal with this client in order to save his business. What are you going to do in this situation? Are you going to persuade the client to do business with you as you would with any other client, not telling about your competitor? Or, are you going to expose the competitor? These are just some of the circumstances when your values will be challenged, where you choose to adhere firmly to what you value, re-examine them or take a whole new direction.

Beware of the ethics gap

The ethics gap is when what you know as right and wrong comes at odds with what needs to be done in order to succeed. Business is full of circumstances that challenge your values and tempt you to abandon them in the pursuit of success.

Removing the gap is next to impossible. There will always be conflicts of interests. The ethical gap can be found in just about any situation. In business, the gap is practically ever present in transactions, negotiations, deals and even in attracting clients. It may also become involved in how you deal with staff, colleagues, customers, business partners, investors, or even family and friends. Everyone has that particular someone they do not want to work or do business with. But there will be circumstances when you will be forced to. The point is not to remove the ethics gap. The challenge is more on reducing the gap.

Reducing the gap requires aligning work principles and values with personal principles and values. Use the result of this alignment when proceeding with the things you have to do.

There are 2 paths you can follow- a negative one and a positive one. Slowly analyze ethics and values. It is crucial to ask yourself if you are willing to go down either the negative path or the positive one. Carefully weigh the pros and cons of each path before you decide. Also, do not forget to take into consideration the effect of your decision on the people around you.

Chapter 33. Establishing Credibility

Being credible greatly helps when negotiating and when you are trying to persuade people. It is an absolute foundation of your capacity to persuade other people. Your negotiating skills are important, but if you are not credible, you would have a hard time persuading others. Do people believe what you tell them? If they don't, then all your efforts will be fruitless. There is absolutely zero chance of persuading other if they do not believe in you- or at least in what you tell them.

People may seem to listen to you, hang on to every word you say. They might spend minutes to hours, even come every day to listen to you. But they won't act unless they believe you. Your ultimate goal in persuading and negotiating is not in getting people to listen. The goal is to get them to act. And for that to happen, you should be able to make them believe in what you tell them. For example, you are talking to clients, trying to get them to place an order or close a deal. You could spend days, or even weeks, negotiating. They can agree to meet you every time you make an appointment. However, they won't sign that deal or place an order unless they believe in you and what you have to offer.

Another example is when you are trying to persuade your staff and your colleagues to implement a new program or make some changes. They may give lip service to all your talk but they won't do what you want them to do unless they believe. You cannot possibly motivate someone who doesn't believe in you. Some may show a little enthusiasm and make some meager efforts in following you. But, half-hearted actions won't help you in achieving your goals.

Parents won't be successful trying to teach their children about things in life if they lack credibility. Most parents tell their children not to do certain things because they don't want their children to make the same mistakes they did. But why do some children refuse to heed parental advice? One likely reason is that they sense that their parents are only trying to manipulate them and that they are only given a portion of the truth.

Whatever the situation, you can make yourself credible with these tips:

Tip #1. Never make an assumption that people do believe in you.

There are 3 main assumptions that highly effective persuaders never make:

1. Assumption on poverty

   Successful persuaders never assume that the other person cannot afford what is being offered to them. Highly effective persuaders always consider each person as capable of availing products and services, regardless of appearances and first impressions. In fact, if persuaded enough, people would use money set aside for basic needs, emergencies or other goals just to get what they are being currently offered. For example, a person can easily use grocery money to purchase an expensive gadget if persuaded enough. A couple would give up their retirement money just to invest in something. A businessman would sell his company just to enter a totally different investment or business venture. Even a school kid will give up his lunch money for something, if persuaded enough. Anyone who is determined to obtain something will find ways to be able to afford it. So, never assume one is too poor for whatever you are offering or selling.

2. Assumption on understanding

Successful persuaders and negotiators never assume that the other person has understood what they were told. People may often show signs of understanding, such as smiling and nodding the head, or making affirmative statements. These are not 100% indicators that the other person has indeed understood what they heard.

To make sure others did understand what you told them, ask. A simple question such as "Did you understand?" or "Is it clear?" helps to establish if the other person has understood. But these are not enough. Some people would answer affirmative to these questions even though they have no clue about they just heard. You need to take a few more steps in order to ascertain understanding. Try these simple techniques:

- Validate by asking leading questions that allow others to make statements based on what they have understood.
- Ask them to rephrase what they heard. This allows the other person to use his own words to explain concepts based on their understanding.
- Ask open-ended questions, which will prompt the other person to state exactly what they have retained from what they have heard.

3. Assumption on believing

   This is the most important assumption never to make. People may have understood you but they may not believe you.

It is upsetting when other people challenge your credibility. It may even cost you your composure and confidence if it happens in public. People dislike even the most simple carding at the bar, getting asked for an ID when entering buildings or when making transactions. It is especially distressing to admit that most people you talk to will be thinking "Really? Can you prove that?"

In business, you can provide a long list of benefits, facts and scientific studies to prove your point. All these will be for nothing if they do not believe you. Sometimes, even the best presentation and the most engaging speaker cannot convince others to act because people do not believe in them.

As a manager, you can talk until you run out of words trying to convince a key employee to stay. You can paint a wonderful future for them if they stay with the company, promise benefits and more opportunities. But you can't persuade them if they do not believe in you. They will not trust you, nor consider the things you are saying if they think you do not have the capacity to make these happen. What you have just said will be empty words to them.

It is inherent for people to be unwilling to find you credible. There will always be some who will not believe you. There will be circumstances when people doubt you and treat your words as empty. This unwillingness to believe stems from years of exposure to advertisements that promise everything, including the moon and the stars. Also, personal experiences of broken trusts, lies, betrayals and being let down all contribute to this hesitation to believe everything. Taking everything at face value is a sure way to disaster, especially in today's world where most people only care for themselves. Disbelief and skepticism are actually tools that help people protect themselves from getting taken advantage of. You need to be aware of this.

As a persuader, your responsibility lies in developing credibility. You should always consider that not everyone will believe you immediately. You should always include how to add credibility to your presentations each and every time. No matter who your target audience is, do not assume that they believe you. You have to always make an effort to be credible.

Tip #2. Tell only as much as people will likely believe

Never tell people more than you think they will believe. Give just enough information to convince them of something. Telling more may cause them to doubt you more than to believe you. Even if what you tell them is the absolute truth, the more information you give, the more likely they are to doubt you. Your chances of persuading them rapidly fails the more you talk. Remember that persuasion is not based on how much you talk but on what you say and how you say it. This may, however require you to give different portions of the entire scenario or different versions of something.

Take for example, talking with a customer about a skin care product. This particular client has expressed that he has tried practically every product there is but his skin problem did not improve. Chances are, he has turned skeptical because of so many failed products. Telling this client your product is revolutionary and contains the latest breakthrough technology to skin care will merely be empty words. He has probably heard these (and several versions of them) before. You won't persuade him with these lines. What you can tell this client, instead, is how your product differs from others. What does your product contain and how it can target specific skin concerns? Some ingredients may be similar to other products. Capitalize on the differences in concentrations. Tell the client that ingredients may be similar but the concentrations differ. This difference determines effectiveness of the product. If you have another client who is practically new to skin care products, the lines "revolutionary, breakthrough technology" may have their intended effect.

Another example is promoting through sales. Having discount sales is a proven technique to attract more customers. However, you can't possibly have too frequent sales because it will lose its appeal. You won't convince customers to "buy now while it is still on sale and get to save more" if they know these same items will be on sale a few days from now. Sears, one of the largest department store chains in America, faced this problem sometime ago. They had sales practically most days of any given week. Instead of attracting more buyers, people bought less because they knew another sale would be up after a few days. Most people preferred to wait a few days before deciding if they will buy an item or not. This prompted the company to resort to adopting a year-round low pricing approach, instead.

Credibility is influenced by the law of diminishing returns. Diminished returns lead to diminished credibility. You are supposed to be excited, talking enthusiastically about whatever it is you are trying to persuade someone. It may be about a service, investment, product, or concept. You should carefully watch your words and the things you disclose. Once your claims or position go beyond your credibility, your chances of persuading others drop rapidly. Stick to the old saying to never mention more than what others are likely to believe.

When you talk too much and your claims become too incredible or as people put it "too good to be true", your credibility drops, too. This is because most people regard such claims as a means of swindling, cheating them of their hard-earned money or getting them to make dubious dealings. Keep your claims within realistic limits, based on the general profile of your audience. Avoid sounding too incredible. Use appropriate words, too. For example, people with scientific backgrounds won't be easily persuaded by words like "revolutionary", "breakthrough", "new formulation", "instant results" etc. These will be interpreted as false claims. These same words will most likely work with people who don't have deep understanding of scientific processes.

Tip #3 Tell the truth

In business, practically everyone is scrambling to prove they are the best; their services and their products are of the highest quality, with no equal. Try a different approach- tell the truth, even if it is ugly.

Take for instance what Doyle, Dane and Bernbach Advertising Agency did with the Volkswagen sedan. This is the car with a round top, a design that remained unchanged for more than twenty years. It looked a beetle or a bug. It was among the ugliest cars that were ever manufactured. It didn't have anything special about it, or any attractive features that advertisers can capitalize on. It didn't even have a gas gauge until after a few years. One would just drive on and on until the gas ran out. When it did, the engine would automatically shift to using gas contained in the reserve tank. This tank was small but contains gas enough to get the car to the next filling station, with a few extra remaining.

Imagine the huge challenge the advertising agency faced when they got this account. They had no special capabilities to highlight. It didn't have anything fancy. It was very simple. In fact, there were only 2 key features- cheap (a full tank can go for lots of miles) and dependable. Everybody who heard about this classic Volkswagen sedan knew these. The ad agency had nothing else to go on. That is, until they decided to tell everybody the truth about the car. Everyone who heard about this plan probably thought the agency was making a suicidal mistake. In an industry that capitalized on highlighting (sometimes, even exaggerating) attractive features, to tell the truth is something unheard of. But the ad agency went ahead with the truth about the car.

The series of ads declared the Volkswagen sedan as "ugly", looking like "bug-a-beetle", "slow", etc. most of the ads played off with the ongoing jokes that people were already telling about the car. The result was totally beyond expectations. Instead of a decline, there was a dramatic increase in sales.

This is just one example of how astoundingly powerful pure and simple truth can be. In a world where people are daily bombarded by falsehoods and half-truths, the truth is pretty much unexpected and makes it a great attention grabber. It helps to make people trust you more because you are not afraid to tell them about your flaws. It also helps if you follow up your truth with a statement to commitment. For example, the same ad agency (Doyle and Dane) used the truth in the Avis rental cars campaign. Instead of going for the usual claim to be the best, largest, etc., the campaign was proud to proclaim the company was "Number Two". The tag line was followed up with a commitment that because they were "number two", they "try harder." A study was in fact made to see if the Avis Company was true to these ads. The number one rental cars company was Hertz and Avis came in second, according to surveys made at that time. Avis employees were indeed trying harder at providing better service. Hertz employees were taking things easy. Some actually felt sympathetic to the underdog position of the Avis employees.

The above examples of truth telling to persuade people and gain credibility revolutionized the advertising world in America. The truth had a very startling effect. Companies were scrambling to create "Doyle and Dane ads". The ad agency created an entirely new advertising method. It became synonymous to truth in advertising. Before these 2 ads, nobody ever considered telling flaws and disadvantages of any product. In fact, efforts were focused on disguising these flaws. Nobody ever spent millions just to tell people that the competitor was better. These 2 ads showed that in the right context and even if painful, telling truth increases credibility and is an amazing, powerful force.

Tip #4 Pointing out disadvantages

Pointing out the disadvantages is a very crucial factor to persuasion. If you do this, you become more believable. Everything you say after pointing out disadvantages is more accepted. This actually has a sound research to back it up. There are 4 rational reasons that this works.

1. It makes other people think that you are objective.

   People expect you to expound on the attractive features and advantages of your service, product, etc. By including the disadvantages, you convey objectiveness. They feel that you are telling them everything they need to know and not just the attractive parts.

2. It complements the listener. They feel you have confidence that they can understand the disadvantages and can make decisions on their own. Because you make them feel good and smart, they can easily be persuaded in your favor.

3. It helps in anticipating objections. By pointing out disadvantages, you are actually limiting objections. You are subconsciously influencing the other person, making him think that the list you have provided are the only ones that should be discussed. Hence, you always have a ready answer. Because you know what objections to expect (based on the disadvantages you disclosed), you can rehearse counter arguments that will win the other person to your proposal.

For example, if you tell potential clients that the disadvantages are A and B, they will no longer think of any other things to object to or question you about. Their mind will be more focused on disadvantages A and B. If inclined, they will more likely question you about these points. You should, of course, have a ready answer for these. This way, you limit any objections, which can catch you off guard and derail your presentation.

4. It gives credibility to all of your other claims.

   People will instantly think you are being honest with them. Everything you say will then be accepted and taken seriously. They will be more open and receptive to your spiel.

Tip #5 Exercise precision with numbers

Numbers are effective tools in persuasion. It provides a sense of firmness and concreteness to something that has yet to be personally proven. People tend to believe and have more confidence in exact numbers than in rounded numbers. That is, they tend to accept precise figures are more realistic.

A precise number would inspire more confidence in the product. Claims such as “99.99% effective against germs” and “99.44% pure” seem more plausible than simply claiming 100%. Nobody is likely to argue with the soap company if they claimed 100% of something about their product. Some companies will put “contains 5% caffeine” or “98% less caffeine” on their labels. Nobody would question and go to great lengths of testing coffee labeled as “Caffeine free”. People will likely believe it anyways. But why go for exact figures? Because it is subliminally considered as more plausible.

In the mind of a person, the exact figures convey that the company went to great lengths, exerted lots of effort and did everything possible before they came up with the figures. It projects an image of crucial and careful study before such exact numbers were obtained, and not just pulling numbers from the air.

Odd figures

Another example is when pricing. Whole figures tend not to sound as firm as when using precise numbers. Noticed that items you buy in groceries and department stores rarely come with whole number process. It is always something like "$10.98", "$0.99" or "$47.35". Larger transactions such as real estate and cars would advertise prices as "$197,000", $3999" or "$268,000". Why can't they just give prices in whole figures such as "$10", "$4000" or "$350,000"? This is often referred to as the "odd figure syndrome", which to include as a technique in persuasion.

Odd figures convey a sense of firmness than exact numbers. Like in the use of precision numbers, odd figures convey the idea that thorough consideration was made before the price was determined. It gives a message that careful scrutiny and all other considerations were addressed. The odd-figured price conveys a message that it is already the most realistic and the lowest possible price that can be given.

Exact Quantities

Numbers provide a more concrete idea. For example, when you market certain software, it is easier to envision a "90% increase in speed" than "double the speed". Exact numbers are more attractive, too. For example, a weight loss pill is more likely to be purchased if it says "reduce your weight by 65%" rather than a mere "lose weight fast."

Conclusion

Thank you again for purchasing this book!

I hope this book was able to help you to learn the fundamental principles of human psychology and specific tactics you can use for manipulation, persuasion and deception. You can use the techniques outlined throughout this book in any situation you find yourself in.

The next step you have to take in your efforts toward using techniques of manipulation, persuasion and deception is to apply this knowledge your everyday life. Be sure to re-read it on a regular basis to remind yourself and make the most of it in your life and achieve your goals faster!

Finally, if you enjoyed this book, please take the time to share your thoughts and post a review on Amazon. We do our best to reach out to readers and provide the best value we can. Your positive review will help us achieve that. It'd be greatly appreciated!

Thank you and good luck!

Check Out My Other Books

Below you'll find some of my other popular books that are popular on Amazon and Kindle as well. Simply click on the links below to check them out. Alternatively, you can visit my author page on Amazon to see other work done by me.

Cure For Controlling People

http://amzn.to/1jGkVBD

ADHD Symptoms & Strategies

http://amzn.to/P4nAtL

Narcissism Unleashed!

http://amzn.to/1jJrinG

Curing Workaholics

http://amzn.to/1pb5O8V

Living With Autism

http://amzn.to/Qibv5h

The Ultimate Self Esteem Guide

http://amzn.to/1tNW4Bm

The Shopping Addiction

http://amzn.to/QIhi4y

Living With OCD

http://amzn.to/1mporll

BOX SET #1 Narcissism Unleashed & Cure For Controlling People

http://amzn.to/1uUGK6o

BOX SET #2 Narcissism Unleashed & Mind Control Mastery

http://amzn.to/1ombagm

BOX SET #3 ADHD Symptoms & Strategies & Living With OCD

http://amzn.to/1uUERXq

BOX SET #4 Living With OCD & Ultimate Self Esteem Guide

http://amzn.to/1slhJNF

BOX SET #5 Living With OCD & Ultimate Self Esteem & Narcissism & Mind Control & Shopping Addiction

http://amzn.to/1ioc84q

BOX SET #6 Ultimate Self Esteem Guide &Narcissism Unleashed

http://amzn.to/ZoDFWN

BOX SET #7 Ultimate Self Esteem Guide & Mind Control Mastery

http://amzn.to/1CaxfDX

If the links do not work, for whatever reason, you can simply search for these titles on the Amazon website to find them.

45978472R00146

Made in the USA
San Bernardino, CA
23 February 2017